# cross
## training

## getting in shape for the race of my life

**MULTNOMAH BOOKS**

CROSS-TRAINING
© 1993 by Questar Publishers, Inc.
published by Multnomah Books
*a part of the Questar publishing family*

*International Standard Book Number: 0-88070-583-3*

Edited by Rodney L. Morris
Cover design by Greg Breeding
Printed in the United States of America.

The publisher gratefully acknowledges permission to use the following copyrighted materials: Chapters 1, 2, 3, and 8 were originally published as DiscipleMaker booklets; chapter 5 is from the book *Decision Making and the Will of God;* chapter 7 is condensed from *Life-Style Evangelism* and *Gentle Persuasion.*

Most Scripture quotations are from the Holy Bible: New International Version,© 1973, 1978, 1984 by International Bible Society.Used by permission of Zondervan Bible Publishers. Scripture quotations in "Worship," chapter 4, are from the Holy Bible, New King James Version, © 1984 by Thomas Nelson, Inc.

For information:
*Questar Publishers, Inc.*
*Post Office Box 1720*
*Sisters, Oregon 97759*

93 94 95 96 97 98 99 00 01 02— 10 9 8 7 6 5 4 3 2 1

# Contents

# Introduction

**H**ave you ever sat on the sidelines watching others do what you knew you could, or should, be doing? What keeps us from stepping out of the bleachers and onto the court or from moving off the sidelines and onto the race track? Many reasons could be offered. But one overly familiar reason often heads the list, whether the activity is playing in a ball game, applying for a promotion at work, or sharing the gospel with a friend or neighbor. The fear of failure.

Fear is a terrible motivator in most situations, but it is particularly inappropriate for Christians who know they are protected by God and that failure need not be permanent. The desire to always work within comfort zones is normal. But our comfort zones must be constantly stretched if we want to grow.

*Cross-Training* is a unique and exciting book that will stretch your spiritual comfort zones. It has been written and published to equip believers around the world for active, effective, Christian living and service.

*Cross-Training* provides eight essential building blocks for living the Christian life as an active participant rather than a casual spectator. Spiritual priorities and the mastery of basic disciplines are needed if we are to aggressively assault the gates of hell rather than be crushed beneath them.

*Cross-Training* is a book about biblical basics for new believers who desire to be equipped to impact this world for Christ. But it is also written for mature believers, focusing on spiritual disciplines and responsibilities we must consistently exercise if we want to be used by God to accomplish his will.

Christians are called by God to be salt and light in this decaying and darkening world. But it is not possible to give what we do not have or share what we do not know. There is a direct correlation between the time we spend in discipleship training and our ability to communicate with others effectively. People all around us are swimming in a sea of moral and ethical relativism. They need help. But few people are willing or able to throw out life lines. As those entrusted with the message of eternal life through Jesus Christ, we must be capable and willing to share more than confusion with those asking questions and seeking answers concerning our hope. This requires a clear understanding of our faith and the ability and willingness to pass on what we have learned.

As ambassadors for Christ our goal for living is neither comfort nor convenience, but rather to be trained instruments in God's hands to help populate heaven and depopulate hell. The Christian life was never intended to be lived in isolation or as a spectator sport. We ought to have more in common with courageous soldiers than with heartless spectators. We have been called to be faithful servants, not pampered aristocrats who expect others to serve us.

## Who will *Cross-Training* appeal to?

*Cross-Training* is an ideal study or discussion book for leadership training, discipling ministries, and small groups, as well as an excellent introduction for new believer classes. It provides concise instruction and encouragement for those seeking practical help in their personal walk with God, and thought-provoking discussion materials for small group studies.

Read the chapter on **God's Word** to find out why reading and studying the Bible is indispensable for anyone who wants to become a disciple of Jesus Christ. If **Scripture Memory** is so important to successful Christian living, how is it done? **Evangelism** will motivate you to consistently share your life and the message of Jesus with others.

Christians often hop across town to find a church distinctly different from the Moose or Elks club. **Fellowship** will show you why people should want to be involved in your church or small group study. Today pantheism, dressed in western clothing, is stealing the minds of non-Christians and Christians alike in far greater numbers than atheism. The issue is no longer the viability of communicating with God; the real issue is which god(s) are we to communicate with. The chapters on **Prayer** and **Worship** describe a communion with God that many individuals desire to experience, but are unsure how to find. Is **Giving** really a responsibility Christians have to take seriously, according to the Bible? Finally, the summary chapter **Discipleship** is for those who obediently step outside of their comfort zones with the gospel. How are we to make disciples of the people who respond positively?

*Cross-Training* addresses each of these topics in a clear, concise fashion that transcends age, gender, and denominational lines. The materials come from the hearts and ministries of men who have field tested what they have written.

Whether you're needing some refresher training in the basics, meeting regularly with a new believer in a disciple-making relationship, or just getting started in this grand adventure of following Christ, this book will help you discover (or rediscover) important disciplines for spiritual growth.

*Cross-Training* is a short book filled with a powerful message. It should be studied, applied, and shared with friends who are interested in preparing for the race of their lives.

Karl I. Payne
for the rest of the *Cross-Training* team

# CHAPTER 1

# God's Word

## *John G. Mitchell*

Years ago I had the opportunity to sit down with G. Campbell Morgan for a few minutes of conversation. Knowing I might never have such an opportunity again with this man who was called "the prince of Bible expositors," I had a question ready for him. "Dr. Morgan, tell me how you study your Bible." He just looked at me. "Mitchell," he finally said, "you wouldn't do it if I told you." "Well," I said, "you try me." He paused a moment, then said, "Before I even start to study a book in the Bible, I read it through forty or fifty times."

He saturated his mind with the Word of God. He let the words of Scripture fill his heart and mind. That was the key to his ministry. Nothing was more important than reading and rereading God's Word.

But why should you and I bother? You may not be a preacher or a teacher, so why should you give yourself to the study of the Scriptures? When you get right down to it, why does it matter whether you and I read our Bibles?

There are many reasons why it matters. As we look together at some of those reasons, we'll soon discover that to read and study God's Word is indispensable for anyone who truly wants to become a disciple of the Lord Jesus.

### The Bible gives us the revelation of God and of his purposes for us.

When you rule out the Bible, you rule out the revelation of God. Where else can you find it? Perhaps you reply,

"Well, I can find God in creation. I can stand on a cliff overlooking the sea or walk along a mountain trail and see what God has created." That may be, but you would still have little idea what God is like.

Creation reveals that God exists and that he is powerful. But what is he like? What sort of God is he? For those answers we must turn to the Word of God. God has communicated to us through that Word and it is there that he reveals both himself and his purposes.

If you rule out the Word of God, you have no revelation about the character, heart, love, grace, and compassion of God. Isn't it wonderful that God should reveal himself to us in his Word?

## The Bible gives us answers for the conditions of our day.

All across this country we can see the breakdown of moral foundations. Why? What's the reason for it? We have ruled out the Word of God. And when you rule out the Scriptures, you rule in lawlessness.

Some years ago I taught a large high school Bible class on Friday afternoons. Youngsters from two high schools made up the class. One Friday I went to class and found that more than half of my students hadn't shown up. After asking around, I found out that the kids who weren't there all came from one high school. I also discovered that one of the teachers at that school discouraged anyone from coming to my class. He had made it almost impossible for them to attend.

About a month after this, I met a teacher from that high school on the street. He stopped me and said, "Mr. Mitchell, what are we going to do about our young people?" He went on to tell me about the growing problems of alcohol and drug abuse and vandalism at the school.

"Sir," I replied, "when we rule the Bible out of our lives, out of our schools and society—even out of some of our churches—we rule in lawlessness."

The Word of God had a prominent role in shaping the

history of both America and Great Britain. In recent years, however, the Bible has been thrown out of the schools, watered down in the churches, and neglected in the home. As a result, we're witnessing a breakup in the very foundation of our national character. What a need there is for us to get back to the Word of God.

The situation in America today makes me think of the nation of Judah during the days of the prophet Jeremiah. God had revealed to the men and women of Judah his person and his character. He had given them his law. The nation was a depository for the Word of God. And when they turned away from the God of their fathers, he sent them prophet after prophet. From early morning until late at night these divine spokesmen poured forth the Word of the Lord, warned the people what would take place if they despised his revelations, and pled with them to turn back. But they would not turn back. They were not eager for the truth, and they went on from evil to evil. These Israelites—the very ones who had been called "God's people"—were ignorant of God.

When you rule out the Word of God, you not only rule in lawlessness, you also rule in ignorance of spiritual realities—ignorance of God, of his person, of his character, and of his work.

### The Bible is authoritative.

What does the Bible have to say about itself? What claims does it make about its own validity and authority?

Jesus told a gathering of Jews, "I tell you the truth, until heaven and earth disappear, not the smallest letter, not the least stroke of a pen, will by any means disappear from the Law until everything is accomplished" (Matt. 5:18). Every detail of God's Word can be counted on. There's no guesswork about it.

This brings me to some special features concerning God's Word, features we can bank our very lives on.

First, *the Bible is God-breathed.* Second Timothy 3:16-17 says: "All Scripture is God-breathed and is useful for teaching, rebuking, correcting and training in righteousness, so that the man of God may be thoroughly equipped for every good work."

The apostle Peter confirms this in his second epistle. There Peter reminds his readers that he had personally seen the glorified Savior on the Mount of Transfiguration. We "were eyewitnesses of his majesty," Peter wrote (1:16). In those amazing moments, Jesus had changed before their very eyes: "His face shone like the sun, and his clothes became as white as the light" (Matt. 17:2).

Now that was a wonderful experience for Peter—the experience of a lifetime. And yet even as he reflects on that special moment he says, "And we have the word of the prophets made *more certain,* and you will do well to pay attention to it" (2 Pet. 1:19).

A "more certain" word? Something even more sure than his experience on the Mount of Transfiguration? What is this "word of the prophets made more certain"? Nothing else but the Word of God. Then Peter adds, "For prophecy never had its origin in the will of man, but men spoke from God as they were carried along by the Holy Spirit" (1:21).

The very words these men wrote were under the inspiration of the Holy Spirit. The whole Bible—from Genesis to Revelation—is equally inspired, the product of divine activity. The men who composed the Scriptures wrote exactly what God wanted them to write. The Spirit took these men and used their individual personalities, their individual gifts and backgrounds, and yet he guided them—even to the very words they would use.

There is a balance here. God did not rule out the unique personalities of these men as they wrote. They were not machines or secretaries taking dictation. You cannot read the Bible without seeing the personalities of the men God used to write it. And yet, though God used men to write the Scriptures, the Word of God has no mistakes; it contains no errors in the original writings. When God gives a revelation, you can bank on it. It is the correct, infallible Word of a holy and righteous God.

And you can bank on another thing. If God has given to us a revelation of himself and of his purposes and program, he's going to guard that revelation. Critics have come and critics have gone. Down through the centuries they have burned the Word of God. They've murdered his servants. They've done their best to rule out the Word of God. But it's still here. And when our present generation of critics has gone off the scene, this Book will still be comforting hearts and leading men and women to the Savior. If the Lord tarries a thousand years, we will have the same revelation from God and people will still be transformed by its living truths.

From the beginning of history, Satan has sought to question God's Word. That was his tactic with Eve. He put a question in her mind as to whether God would keep his Word, as to whether he meant what he said. That was the tempter's tactic at the dawn of time, and it's still his tactic today.

My friend, the world may pass away. This generation may pass away. But the Word of God will never pass away. We can bank on that. The Bible speaks with all the authority of the living God.

When I think of the arrogance of humankind today and the opposition to the Bible, I am so happy that we have a revelation from God that is just as eternal as the living God himself. No generation on earth is going to destroy the Bible. As the psalmist says:

Your word, O LORD, is eternal;
　　it stands firm in the heavens (Psa. 119:89).

God's Word has been underwritten by his very name, and it is authoritative in every department of the believer's life.

Some people are thankful for and glory in experiences in their Christian life. I am not opposed to experiences—God forbid—if they are right experiences. But these must be judged in the light of God's Word. Experiences are passing things; the Word of God is established forever,

The Bible is the cornerstone upon which our faith must rest. We dare not ignore it. We dare not be ignorant of it.

## The Bible meets our every spiritual need.

God uses his Word in people's lives. We may talk of methods of study or methods of teaching, but if people's lives are changed they are changed because God has been pleased to use his Word. As Paul says in 1 Thessalonians 1:5, "Our gospel came to you not simply with words, but also with power, with the Holy Spirit and with deep conviction.."

I am reminded too of the first psalm, a psalm which accurately depicts the character of our Lord. The psalm begins, "Blessed is the man," and proceeds to tell us three things about that man:

Blessed is the man
    who does not walk in the counsel of the wicked
or stand in the way of sinners
    or sit in the seat of mockers.
But his delight is in the law of the LORD,
    and on his law he meditates day and night.

Surely our Savior was a "blessed man" who meditated on God's Word "day and night." And if the Lord found time to do that with the busy life he lived among men, there's no excuse for you or me neglecting the Word of God. I know you're busy. All of us are. Sometimes I think we are too busy. Sometimes we are even too busy in the service of the Lord, and there is a danger we may grow slack in our commitment to the Word of God itself.

Psalm 19 speaks even more about how the Bible meets spiritual needs. In the first six verses we see the revelation of God *in creation.* Then in verse seven through the end of the psalm, we have the revelation of God *in his Word.* That Word is "perfect, trustworthy, right, radiant, pure, sure and altogether righteous." Then the psalmist concludes with this marvelous description of the surpassing value of God's Word:

They are more precious than gold,
   than much pure gold;
they are sweeter than honey,
   than honey from the comb.
By them is your servant warned;
   in keeping them there is great reward. (vv. 10-11)

Although God's glory is revealed through his creative acts, it's when you come to the Word of God that you get down to business with God himself. The Word is pure and clean. It opens your eyes, cleanses your life, and fills your heart with joy.

### The Bible is inexhaustible in its truths

What do I mean by inexhaustible? I mean the Bible is always new. It always satisfies. Did you ever stop to consider the amazing variety of people from all over the world, with so many different backgrounds and cultures, who come to the Word of God and are satisfied. The babe in Christ can read it and get blessed. The seasoned saint can read it and get blessed. You can work your way through a whole book or take a verse and pull it to pieces. It's inexhaustible.

I've been reading and studying the Word of God for more than sixty years, and I'll tell you very honestly, I've barely scratched the surface. You could study your Bible every day, sunup to sundown, for a lifetime and you'd just be making a start. This Book was written by the living God, and he has given it to you and me!

Perhaps you say, "Sometimes I read my Bible and get nothing out of it." That may be true. God never promised to reveal his truths wholesale to us when we come to his Word. We must come to the Word day after day, reading it over and over, so that we may begin to grow in the truth.

You may say, "But I get tired of reading and rereading." And so you skim the Bible. Don't do it! The Bible deserves to be read word for word. It's inexhaustible. You can never plumb the depths of this amazing Book because it's God-breathed. If you could plumb the depths of an almighty, sovereign, living God, you could plumb the depths of the Bible. It's his very Word.

## The Bible presents the supreme character of Jesus Christ.

An unbeliever was constantly ridiculing Christians and their belief in the Bible. Finally one man was so disturbed by the taunts that he said to the unbeliever, "Did you ever sit down and read about Jesus Christ? I suggest you take time to read through the Gospels before you criticize anymore."

The unbeliever accepted the man's challenge. He borrowed a Bible, went home, and read straight through Matthew, Mark, Luke, and John. The next time he met the Christian man who challenged him, he said, "If Jesus Christ is not God, then the man who wrote those words must have been God." No human mind could have conceived such a personality, such an individual as Jesus Christ.

If you find that statement difficult to believe, then take some time yourself to read through the four Gospels. Too many Christians, unfortunately, have not read through these books. We read a few verses in John one day, and then the next day a few verses from the Psalms. Why not read a book through? Open your heart and mind and let the truth of the Gospels grip your life anew. Read them over and over until you're full of the words and acts of the Savior. If the Spirit of God is going to bring change and growth into your life, he must have something to work on. And the tools he uses to change our lives are all from the Word of God.

I urge you to get on your knees before the Lord and ask the Spirit of God to reveal the very thoughts of the living God to you. He will do it. If you're wondering where to start, I suggest the Gospels. Keep reading until you fall in love with Jesus Christ all over again.

## The Bible reveals God's plan of redemption.

The Bible tears the cover off the heart of man and then tells him how he can come into the very presence of God. If you want a picture of your heart as it appears before God, read your Bible. Scripture gives us an accurate picture of what we are in our sins, in our helplessness, in our hopelessness. If it just stopped there, we'd be in trouble. But it doesn't. The Bible doesn't leave us in our despair. Shining forth from its pages is the Lord's wonderful plan to redeem us.

The Word of God shows us the way of salvation. And it's so simple. John 3:36 says, "Whoever believes in the Son has eternal life, but whoever rejects the Son will not see life, for God's wrath remains on him."

There is nothing complicated about it. In John 8:24 Christ says, "If you do not believe that I am the one I claim to be, you will indeed die in your sins." But then in verse 51 of the same chapter he says, "I tell you the truth, if anyone keeps my word, he will never see death." There is the contrast, the clear choice between darkness and light, between death and eternal life.

"Salvation is found in no one else," Peter told the rulers of Israel, "for there is no other name under heaven given to men by which we must be saved" (Acts 4:12).

"I am the gate," Jesus said. "Whoever enters through me will be saved." And, "I am the way and the truth and the life. No one comes to the Father except through me" (John 10:9; 14:6).

The New Testament casts light after light on the path of salvation. Again and again it explains how sinful men and women, through simple faith, can come into a right relationship with the living God.

### The Bible is the source of life.

When I say the Bible is the source of life, I'm talking about spiritual life, eternal life, indwelling life, satisfying life, resurrection life. These are the very terms used in the New Testament. In John 20:30-31, for example, the apostle writes:

> Jesus did many other miraculous signs in the presence of his disciples, which are not recorded in this book. But these are written that you may believe

that Jesus is the Christ, the Son of God, and that by believing *you may have life* in his name.

Our Lord said in John 6:63, "The words I have spoken to you are spirit and they are life." The Bible brings life to the man or woman who will accept the Savior. For "in him is life," and when I come into right relationship with Jesus Christ through his Word, I receive eternal life, resurrection life...incorruptible life.

Peter affirms this in 1 Peter 1:23, where he says that we have been "born again, not of perishable seed, but of imperishable, through the living and enduring word of God."

All over the world, wherever the Word of God is available in the language of the people, men and women come to the Savior and find life. This is a staggering thought! Some of the wisest and most intelligent men in the world, as well as some of the poorest, most ignorant men in the world, have found common ground in the Word of God. Regardless of their cultures, backgrounds, nationalities, or occupations, they have all found real life, real satisfaction, peace of heart, and peace of mind in Christ Jesus.

You simply can't afford to live in the world and not know something of the Word of God. What do you know about the Savior with whom you are going to live eternally? I want to know him, don't you? I am going to spend eternity with him, not just three score and ten years here on earth.

It doesn't matter how long you have been a Christian—ten days or ten years—you cannot grow in your spiritual life nor in the power of God without dipping your empty cup into the Word of Truth.

### The Bible offers guidelines for life.

In a world full of lawlessness and corruption, in a day of crumbling morals and shifting foundations, we need guidelines for living. How can I live in such an age as this when everything is falling apart? How can I get along when society grows more lawless, more corrupt, and more sinful with each passing day? Psalm 119:105 has an encouraging answer:

Your word is a lamp to my feet
and a light for my path.

Isn't that wonderful? The Spirit of God through the Word of God will guide you through the shoals, quicksand, storms, sorrows, and afflictions of life.

"But I fall so much," you say. Yes, and so do I. But the Bible gives provision for our failures. The Bible is a moral cleanser. John Bunyan wrote in the fly leaf of his Bible, "This Book will keep me from sin, but sin will keep me from this Book."

I've seen this confirmed time and again. As a pastor I've dealt with hundreds upon hundreds of people who have fallen out of fellowship with the Savior. I always ask them the same question: "What was the first step in your departure from God and fellowship with him?" I nearly always receive the same answer: "We began to neglect the Word of God."

You cannot ignore and neglect the Bible without feeling the effects of that neglect on your life. In Psalm 119:9-11 the writer declares:

How can a young man keep his way pure?
By living according to your word.
I seek you with all my heart;
do not let me stray from your commands.
I have hidden your word in my heart
that I might not sin against you.

The Bible, like no other book in the world, has the power to keep your life clean.

A few years ago at a Bible conference in the Midwest, I met a young man from New York City whose life had been a living tragedy. He had been in and out of jails and penitentiaries again and again. He had robbed people to support his drug habit and led his own street gang. But once when he was sitting in a jail cell, someone gave him a Bible, and he came to know Jesus Christ as his Savior—right in that dirty cell.

"Mr. Mitchell," he told me, "when I came out of that jail I didn't have any idea which way to turn. But I knew one thing. I was through with dope and all the rest of it. The Lord had really saved me. I was clean."

Now, every chance he gets, he goes back to those jails to tell the inmates how his life was transformed by Jesus Christ. He came into contact with the living Word by reading the written Word.

The Word of God has power to change the course of your life. Years and years ago it got a hold on my life, and it has been working on me ever since. It can be the same for you. Your life can be transformed. Not only does the Word have power to guide you from darkness into light, it can also show you where and how to walk through life each day.

If your heart is open and you're ready to accept what the Spirit of God has to say to you, God will take his Word and make it real to you. But you have to be open. You have to mean business. If you do, he's ready and more than willing to meet you in your need.

### The Bible gives us confidence to face the future.

The Scriptures give wonderful hope to the believer. How well I know that. During my years in the pastorate, I spent time with many dear people who were ready for glory, ripe for heaven. Hope? I should say so. Standing on the very edge of death, their lives were overflowing with hope. A number of them used to tell me, "Don't feel sorry for me, Brother Mitchell. And don't you pray for me to stay on down here. I want to go home."

The Word of God gives us that hope.

"In my Father's house are many rooms; if it were not so, I would have told you. I am going there to prepare a place for you. And if I go and prepare a place for you, I will come back and take you to be with me that you also may be where I am" (John 14:2-3).

It's always nice to go home. And when you get to heaven, Christian friend, you've just gone home. It's a wonderful thing to have a home—an eternal home—to which you can go.

The Word of God reveals the destination of those who have trusted in Christ.

The Word of God has also revealed the destination of those who have never trusted in Christ. Men are saved through the Word of God. But men are also judged by the Word of God. If sinners are saved by the Word of God—the Spirit of God using the Word in open hearts—that same Word brings judgment on the one who rejects the revelation.

The Bible tells us that the unsaved are going to be raised from the dead, but they will be raised for judgment. As our Lord said, every idle word is going to come into judgment. Unless you have been cleansed by the blood of Christ, unless you have been brought into right relationship with the Savior, you will have to stand before Jesus Christ. And he will be your Judge. The very One you rejected, the One you laughed about, scorned, and spurned...he will be your Judge. John 5:22 says, "The Father judges no one, but has entrusted all judgment to the Son, that all may honor the Son just as they honor the Father."

Scripture is absolutely clear on this point: Every one of us must stand before the Son of God. If we have received him by faith, he will be our Savior. He'll be there to welcome us home. If we have turned him away, he will be our final Judge.

## Make it your own

What you are in your life day by day will be determined by what place you give to the Word of God. I challenge you to read it, appropriate it, make it your own. Read your Bible in such a way that you hear God speaking to you.

And as we read the Word of God, he does speak to us. Isn't it wonderful that in this blessed Book he not only reveals his person and his character, he also reveals his limitless provision for our lives? It's a provision that gives us eternal salvation, that keeps us daily from sin, and that gives us the incomparable hope that one of these days we're going to see him face to face. And when we see him, we shall be just like him (1 John 3:2-3).

This hope is based on the faithfulness of God to keep his Word. It does not depend on your faithfulness or my faithfulness. If it depended on us, we'd never make it. We'd be damned eternally. But our gracious God has made promise after promise to us; he's gone on record in his Word, and we can bank our lives on what he has said.

So why don't we get into the Bible? Why don't we read it, reread it, and meditate on its truths? Meditation is similar to rumination, which simply means to "chew the cud." When a cow chews the cud, she chews up a mouthful of grass, swallows it, and then sometime later she brings it up again and chews on it some more. Eventually the cow receives all the benefit she can from that mouthful of grass, and she stops chewing on it.

Not so with the Word of God. You can never, never chew all the good out of it. You can never exhaust the truths God has revealed. So take a word, a phrase, a verse, a paragraph, a chapter, or a book and chew on it awhile. Think about it later and chew on it some more. Feed on it all you can, as often as you can. Let those words of Scripture flavor every thought, every activity, and every relationship in your life.

The trouble with most of us Christians is we already know these things. We believe the Bible. We agree that we should study God's Word. We're convinced that knowledge of the Scriptures is vital to the Christian walk. We would even concur that ignorance of the Bible among God's people is nothing less than a tragedy. But if we believe all this, then why in the world don't we get down to business and start reading our Bibles? Why are we so casual about it? Why don't we read like our lives depended on it?

Let's get busy and do it. Let's get a firm grip on God's will for our lives, and let's take time now and then to fill our thoughts with heaven.

When it comes time for me to leave one of these days, I know where I'm going. My Bible tells me that I'm going home. I'm going to see the One who died for me—face to face. This is the hope he's given to us in his Word. We will spend eternity in unbroken, wonderful fellowship with him.

Doesn't that whet your appetite to begin enjoying fellowship with him even now? That fellowship is waiting for us if we will but spend time in his Word. Let's get busy and read that Book!

## CrossCheck

1. "To read and study God's Word is indispensable for anyone who truly wants to become a disciple of the Lord Jesus." Agree or disagree? Why?

2. The author gives several reasons why it matters whether or not we read our Bibles. Which of those reasons do you find the most compelling?

3. The author says, "The Bible is the cornerstone upon which our faith must rest." What do you think he means by that statement?

4. If the Bible is all that we claim it to be, why don't we spend more time reading, studying, and meditating on it?

5. How close are you to being able to say, with the psalmist, that God's Word is more precious than "much pure gold"?

John G. Mitchell founded Multnomah School of the Bible (now Multnomah Bible College) in Portland, Oregon, in 1936. He was a member of the first graduating class of Dallas Theological Seminary (1927) and was pastor of Portland's Central Bible Church from 1931 to 1968.

# CHAPTER 2

# Scripture Memory

## *James Braga*

*"Every Christian who wants his life to count for God should memorize Scripture."* This is what I was taught in a class in personal evangelism shortly after I began my training in Bible school. So I threw myself into the task. Within a few weeks I had learned thirty verses. But by the time I reached forty verses, I had forgotten several of the ones I had learned earlier; the more new verses I memorized, the more of the former ones slipped from memory. I gave up at the end of the semester. Before completing Bible school I tried again, only to fail once more.

Still, I could not forget the profound impression my teacher left upon me. That man of God memorized a verse of Scripture every day. Through his ability to quote from the Bible, he was used by God to win countless people to Christ. So I prayed. I asked the Lord to show me how I could memorize Scripture. He answered by helping me discover an easy method for memorizing *and retaining* many, many verses.

Because the Lord enabled me to memorize much of his Word, I know he can do the same for you. This chapter will explain some basic procedures to help you memorize the Word of God. These instructions are simple, and if you will prayerfully follow this program with patience and persistence, you too will soon be able to quote large numbers of verses from the Bible. Scripture memorizing will eventually become a delightful habit, and the rewards will be beyond your comprehension. But before we look at the "how to" of memorizing Scripture, we need to remind ourselves of some of the reasons it is so important.

## The Importance of Memorizing Scripture

The value of memorizing Scripture can never be overestimated. It is one of the essentials of the Christian life. Charles Swindoll writes, "No other single practice in the Christian life is more rewarding, practically speaking, than memorizing Scripture....No other single discipline is more useful and rewarding than this. No other single exercise pays greater spiritual dividends." Consider a few of the benefits:

*1. The memorized Word promotes spiritual growth.* Nothing is more important to a believer than his spiritual development. Filling your heart and mind with Scripture enables you to "grow in the grace and knowledge of our Lord and Savior Jesus Christ." As you have a quiet moment during the day or a wakeful hour at night, a verse or two of Scripture can become the focus of meditation and communion with God.

At the beginning of Joshua's career as the leader of the people of Israel, the Lord said to him, "Do not let this Book of the Law depart from your mouth; meditate on it day and night, so that you may be careful to do everything written in it. Then you will be prosperous and successful" (Josh. 1:8). Joshua's success was dependent upon his meditation on and obedience to God's Word. The same holds true for us, and as we will soon discover, memorizing Scripture and meditating on God's Word go hand in hand.

*2. The memorized Word cleanses the believer.* Interceding with his Father on behalf of his disciples, the Lord Jesus prayed: "Sanctify them by the truth; your word is truth" (John 17:17). It is through the Word of God that the believer is cleansed. In memorizing Bible verses, the Scriptures become the instrument through which the mind is renewed and the heart cleansed. For this reason the psalmist declared:

> I have hidden your word in my heart
> that I might not sin against you. (Psa. 119:11)

*3. The memorized Word is a source of assurance and comfort.* Every believer faces times of crisis and need. Emergencies arise that baffle or overwhelm us. At times like these, the Word of God stored away in the mind and heart can become our solace and strength.

A few years ago the pastor of an evangelical church in a totalitarian state was thrown into prison and required to attend indoctrination classes several hours each day. Late one night he and several other prisoners were called out of their cells and told they had to renounce Christianity. They all knew that if they said the wrong thing, it could mean severe punishment, even death. One man, though he believed in God, cowered under scrutiny and denied his faith.

Before the time came for the pastor to give his answer, he looked up in silent prayer to God for wisdom and help. Immediately a passage he had learned long before came to mind: "You will be brought before kings and governors, and all on account of my name. This will result in your being witnesses to them. But make up your mind not to worry beforehand how you will defend yourselves. For I will give you words and wisdom that none of your adversaries will be able to resist or contradict" (Luke 21:12-15). Then with quiet confidence he stood and spoke. He denounced liberalism and those who claimed to be Christians but denied the Word of God and the deity of the Lord Jesus. Wonderfully his answer fully satisfied his interrogators. The memorized Scriptures had become his strong support at the very moment he needed it, and the Lord proved, as he had done many times previously, that he is faithful to his promises.

*4. The memorized Word equips for effective witnessing.* We cannot adequately present the claims of Christ to the unsaved without using the Bible. To explain the gospel successfully to an unregenerate individual, we must be able to recite key verses without hesitation and must also know where those verses are located in the Scriptures.

An unbeliever once attended an evangelistic meeting to harass the preacher. At the close of the service he engaged the evangelist in an argument, but every time he raised a point of contention, the evangelist answered with a pertinent Scripture. The following day one of the unbeliever's friends noticed that he looked crestfallen and questioned him about his confrontation with the evangelist. He answered, "I did not realize that I was trying to argue with God Almighty." The words of Scripture had pierced the unbeliever to his heart; he was convicted of sin and later trusted Christ as his Savior.

Hebrews 4:12 says: "The word of God is living and active. Sharper than any double-edged sword, it penetrates even to dividing soul and spirit, joints and marrow; it judges the thoughts and attitudes of the heart." How important therefore to quote the actual words of Scripture rather than using our own words to lead people to Christ.

5. *The memorized Word is a means of edifying others.* In these desperate days, people need the encouragement and comfort only the Bible can give. As we relate portions of the memorized Word to them, we speak "what is helpful for building others up according to their needs" (Eph. 4:29). And as we pass on words that "benefit those who listen," we likewise are built up in the faith.

But though many Christians are aware of the rewards of memorizing God's truth, few ever take up the challenge to do it. Some simply procrastinate, thinking they will get to it some day. Others really want to memorize Scripture but have no idea how to do it successfully. Still others have attempted to memorize God's Word, but since they lacked a way to retain the few verses they did memorize, they soon gave up. If any of these situations describe you, take heart. There is a way to successfully memorize God's Word and to enjoy the rewards that memorizing Scripture brings.

## The Card System of Memorizing Scripture

Memory cards provide the most effective way to memorize Scripture. The following steps for using the card system call for self-discipline, but they are a proven method of learning to memorize the Word of God.

*1. Write the verses to be memorized on cards you can carry with you.* You can purchase printed cards with selected Scripture verses from a Bible bookstore, but if you are going to learn many verses, it is preferable to buy a pack of three-by-five cards and make a set of your own. You can carry these wherever you go. Write or type the full quotation of each text on one side of the card and the reference on the other. If you can write small, cut the cards in half. Smaller cards fit more easily into your purse or pocket. For ease of handling, the cards should be uniform in size. Bind the cards together with a rubber band so they won't scatter.

In selecting verses to be memorized, choose those that arrest your attention. You will also want to memorize texts on salvation to use when explaining the gospel to the unconverted. Many find it helpful to memorize verses on topics such as assurance, guidance, comfort, temptation, grace, and victory. Besides memorizing verses on many different topics, it is often advantageous to learn an entire psalm or chapter in the Bible. Many Christians like to memorize a whole book such as Ephesians, 1 and 2 Timothy, or even Romans.

Chet Bitterman, Bible translator with Wycliffe, memorized 1 Peter, a book written to encourage early Christians undergoing persecution for their faith. Little did Chet realize how much those verses would mean to him. In 1981, he was kidnapped by terrorists in Colombia and held for five weeks before they killed him. While in captivity he was able to get a message to his wife, in which he quoted 1 Peter 3:15-16: "Always be prepared to give an answer to everyone who asks you to give the reason for the hope that you have. But do this with gentleness and respect, keeping a clear conscience, so that those who speak maliciously against your good behavior in Christ may be ashamed of their slander." No doubt these

Scriptures gave him the guidance and help he needed, not only in writing to his wife but also in dealing with the terrorists through all the harrowing days before his murder.

*2. Note the context of each verse.* When we read an isolated text in the Bible, we are likely to misunderstand the real meaning of the verse. For instance, Matthew 6:6 reads, "But when you pray, go into your room, close the door and pray to your Father, who is unseen. Then your Father, who sees what is done in secret, will reward you." If we memorize this verse without first noting the context, we might think the Lord was emphasizing secrecy in prayer. A glance at the preceding verse reveals that the Lord was teaching not secrecy but sincerity in prayer. Always seek to understand the verse you wish to memorize by first observing its context.

*3. Read your memory cards.* Do not try to memorize a verse every day. Instead, take your memory cards wherever you go and simply read them repeatedly every day. After you have read each verse, turn the card over and note the reference on the other side. When you have gone over all your cards, reverse the procedure by checking each reference first and then attempting to recall the quotation on the other side. Do this as frequently as you can. Learning the reference at the same time as you memorize the verse will associate the two together in your mind. Then when you read or hear the words of the text or hear the reference cited, you will be able to connect the verse and its reference.

*4. Set aside a regular time each day to go over your cards.* Successful Scripture memorizing requires systematic effort. For many, the best time is in the early morning when the mind is fresh and free from distraction. For others, the best time is just before going to bed. Besides these specific times, utilize your spare moments when riding on a bus or plane, during an interval in your daily routine, or while waiting to be served in a restaurant. If you follow these first four steps every day, some of the verses together with their references will fasten themselves in your memory. What might have seemed an impossibility before will have become an accomplished fact without any stressful effort. Furthermore, you will have the joy of realizing that you have begun to equip yourself to be an instrument of blessing to others.

5. *Memorize each verse thoroughly.* Make sure you can quote word for word the verse on each card and can state the reference correctly. Only after you are certain you have mastered a verse and its reference should you remove the card from the set you carry about every day. As you lay aside the cards you have thoroughly memorized (more about these cards in a moment), add new ones to the pack you carry all the time. Here are some tips to help you memorize your verses thoroughly:

• Write the verse down again and again. Observing the words as well as copying the verse by hand will make an indelible impression. To save time, abbreviate many of the words as you copy the text.

• Whisper the verse to yourself or say it out loud.

• Hand your cards to a friend and ask him to check you as you quote the verses and references.

• Record some of your verses and their references and listen to them in your spare time.

As you become more practiced in memorizing Scripture, you will probably discover additional memory aids to help you learn your verses thoroughly and in less time.

### Retaining the Verses You've Memorized

The key to memorizing Scripture and retaining what you've memorized is to systematically review the verses you've learned. Unless you go over them from time to time, many will soon slip from your mind. In order to retain these verses, you need to initiate a plan for reviewing them regularly. Here s how to do it.

1. *Maintain a systematic review.*

*Weekly Review.* Once you've mastered some of the verses on the cards you carry every day, remove those cards and place them in a second set of cards for review once a week.

Set aside a day each week for this review and keep this schedule faithfully. Go over all the cards to be reviewed weekly, reciting the quotation and then the reference and vice versa. If after a week you have forgotten either the quotation or its reference, return the card to the daily pack. Be strict with yourself. Do not allow a single card to pass unless you are sure you can state the quotation and reference perfectly and without hesitation.

*Semimonthly Review.* Once you know a verse and its reference well enough that you no longer need to go over it weekly, set that card aside for a semimonthly review. Fix two days in the month for this semimonthly review, say the first and the fifteenth of each month. As with the weekly review, try to maintain a regular schedule for these reviews. As you consistently review your memory cards, you will find that some of the cards you read every day may be passed from the daily into the weekly review and others from the weekly to the semimonthly review. Within a month you will have three sets of cards: your daily, your weekly, and your semimonthly reviews.

*Monthly Review.* The verses for the monthly review are the ones you have learned so well you do not need to go over them twice every month. As in the previous reviews, choose a fixed day for this exercise and stick to it.

By this time you will have four sets of cards: the daily, weekly, semimonthly, and monthly. If you are careful to carry out this routine, the number of verses you are committing to memory will soon be considerable. The more verses you learn, the more important it will be to check them over regularly.

*Quarterly Review.* The verses you set aside for quarterly review are those you have come to know so well that you no longer need to go over them once a month. The quarterly review ensures that you are still able to recall both the text and the reference of each verse. Should you have problems recalling either, return that memory card to one of the sets you review more frequently, such as the weekly or even the daily review if necessary.

*Semiannual Review.* When the time comes for this

review, the verses and their references will have become so familiar that you will be able to quote each verse with its reference instantly. In time, you will have learned a number of verses so thoroughly they will be stored permanently in your memory bank.

Throughout these reviews, keep adding new verses to your daily cards and moving other cards from one review to another as the verses become more and more fixed in your mind. Whenever you fail to recall a reference or are unable to repeat a verse correctly from any one of the reviews, place the card back where you began and take it up the line of reviews all over again. To keep the cards that belong to each level of review from getting mixed up, file them in a box using labeled index tabs to keep each grouping separate.

This system of review may sound like a lot of work, and it does require you to invest some time and effort. But if you carry out these instructions resolutely, your efforts will be crowned with success.

### 2. Be fully committed to this task.

Many start out with great enthusiasm to memorize the Word of God but do not continue with it. They learn a number of verses, but after a time they become discouraged and give up. Perhaps they fail to realize that memorizing Scripture is a spiritual work. In seeking to implant God's truth in their hearts, they are engaged in a spiritual conflict. To enter this arena with a half-hearted attitude will not suffice. Difficulties and interruptions are certain to arise. If we are to counter the obstacles that confront us, we must from the outset be determined to follow through, come what may.

### 3. Pray it through.

Our adversary, the devil, knows that the Christian who memorizes Scripture may some day become a mighty instrument for God. Satan will do everything in his power to thwart our efforts. We are no match for such a ruthless foe, but as we pray persistently about our desire and commitment to memorize God's Word, the Lord will enable us to succeed.

# The Practical Use of the Memorized Word

*1. Put the Scriptures you have memorized to use your life.*

The most valuable use you can make of the verses you have learned is to apply them to your walk with the Lord. Only after the Word of God has become a part of you through prayerful meditation and personal application can you ever hope to become an instrument of blessing to others.

Meditation cannot be done in a hurry. It is that quiet and deep reflection upon the Scriptures which allows the Spirit of God to open the mind and heart to what he wants to say. When we meditate on a passage we've memorized, we go over the portion of Scripture again and again, conversing with ourselves as we ponder the text. We consider it from one angle and then from another.

Take Psalm 23:1 for an example: "The LORD is my shepherd, I shall not be in want." In meditating on this verse I ask myself what the word *shepherd* means. Several ideas come to my mind. A shepherd guides, protects, tends, and provides for his sheep. But the psalmist declares that he has no ordinary shepherd. His shepherd is none other than the Lord.

Musing further upon the text, I observe that the psalmist did not write, "The LORD is *a* shepherd." Instead he writes, "The LORD is *my* shepherd," claiming this mighty and caring shepherd as his own. David's shepherd was equal to any need, any problem, any circumstance, any enemy. No wonder David could exclaim, "I shall not be in want."

Can I truly say that this same shepherd is my personal shepherd? If I can, why do I not trust him with my needs and cares? Is he not able to deal with my present circumstances as he did for his people long ago? If my eyes were on my shepherd, I too ought to be able to say, "I shall not be in want." If not, what is the reason for my lack of confidence?

But when David speaks of the Lord being his shepherd, he implies that he is the Lord's sheep. In the same way, if I claim him to be my shepherd, I am likening myself to a sheep, *his* sheep. This makes me think of the characteristics of sheep. Sheep are weak, defenseless, senseless, easily led astray, and in need of constant care, protection, and provision. How well aware I am that this is an apt description of me, and it causes me to appreciate my shepherd all the more.

Then I recall John 10:11 where Jesus says: "I am the good shepherd. The good shepherd lays down his life for the sheep." And I am one of his sheep—albeit a poor, weak, foolish, and needy sheep for whom he gave his life. So my heart rises up in praise.

Thus meditation may lead to heart searching, confession, and repentance. It will also promote prayer and renewal of spirit, as well as thanksgiving and praise.

Meditation does not have to be confined to the prayer closet. It can be done anywhere and at any time, provided my mind is free and able to concentrate. Repeating the verse to ourselves and praying for the Holy Spirit to illuminate the text, we can then begin to muse on the truth. Remember Philippians 4:8, "Whatever is true, whatever is noble, whatever is right, whatever is pure, whatever is lovely, whatever is admirable—if anything is excellent or praiseworthy—think about such things." In this way we fulfill Paul's admonition, "Let the word of Christ dwell in you richly" (Col. 3:16).

Storing Scripture in the mind, together with meditation on it, must be followed by obedience to what God says. Yieldedness to the Spirit of God is indispensable if my life is to be blessed by him. Our lives should be characterized by submission to all that the Lord commands. Such a life of wholehearted commitment does not come easily, but it is the only way to true and lasting blessing.

As we apply the memorized Word to ourselves, we can then expect the Lord to use us in his service. It is for this reason that the Holy Spirit declares through the apostle Paul, "All Scripture is God-breathed and is useful for teaching, rebuking, correcting and training in righteousness, *so that the man of God may be thoroughly equipped for every good work*" (2 Tim. 3:16-17).

Jacob DeShazer was one of several U.S. airmen shot down during the first bombing of Tokyo in World War II. After several months in captivity, Jacob's captors allowed him the loan of a Bible for three weeks. Although DeShazer had been reared in a Christian home, he had never regarded the claims of Christ seriously. But when the Bible was brought to him, he devoured its contents. As soon as there was enough light to see, Jacob read and read, hour after hour, day after day. He read the Scriptures through several times.

As DeShazer read, he finally realized he was a guilty sinner in the sight of a holy God. He realized too that his guilt had been paid for by Jesus Christ. There alone in his prison cell DeShazer took God at his Word and trusted in Christ as his Savior. He was so overjoyed that he later declared, "I would not have exchanged places with anyone at that time."

DeShazer decided to memorize as much of the Bible as he could. As a result of meditating on the Word, he understood that because he was now a Christian, the Lord expected obedience from him, including loving his enemies. Shortly afterward DeShazer faced a real test. One morning, when Jacob was being returned to his cell after a few minutes of exercise, the guard intentionally slammed the cell door on Jacob's foot. Jacob was filled with bitter resentment toward the guard, but just then Matthew 5:44 came forcibly to his mind, "I say unto you, Love your enemies, and pray for them that persecute you." Jacob recognized that this was a challenge from the Lord to submit to him.

Jacob had learned a little Japanese by that time, and when the guard appeared the next morning, Jacob surprised him with a courteous greeting. The amazed captor soon recognized an extraordinary change in his prisoner. As time went on, the guard's attitude toward Jacob also changed. Instead of treating him harshly, he extended special favors to him. Jacob learned that to love his enemy as the Lord teaches us was the best way to act toward his fellow man.

DeShazer was held for fourteen months in solitary confinement after he became a Christian, and the verses he had stored in his memory became his strength and comfort. Jacob sensed that the Lord had called him to bring the gospel some day to the Japanese. Two months after his release and return to the United States, Jacob enrolled in a Bible college to prepare for service as a missionary to Japan. When he returned to Japan four years later, many people went to hear him preach, and two of his former prison guards responded to the call for salvation.

Who can tell the blessing that can come from the prayers of godly parents, from the reading of the Bible, from believing the Word of God, from the memorizing of the Scriptures, and then from walking in the light of this Book?

*2. Proclaim the memorized Word to the unsaved.*

When your mind and heart are filled with the Word, you will want to talk about the Good News of salvation wherever you go, for the Lord has said, "Out of the overflow of the heart the mouth speaks" (Matt. 12:34). There are all kinds of ways of doing this.

A Christian student who thumbed through his memory cards while riding on a commuter train took advantage of an innate human trait. Often the person sitting next to him would be curious about what he was doing and would sometimes even lean over to discover what was written on the cards. So this student prepared a special set of cards with brief but pointed verses in large, clear script specially designed for any inquisitive passenger. The train was frequently crowded and noisy, but the young man found that he could communicate the gospel to any curious commuter.

*3. Proclaim the memorized Word to other Christians.*

The memorized Word could extend your ministry and pay incalculable spiritual dividends. It may edify the saints as you quote the Scriptures when you pray in public; it will encourage the sick when you bring them a suitable portion of the Word; it will comfort those who are going through trials "with the comfort we ourselves have received from God." Not only so, a text fitly spoken in ordinary conversation with a fellow believer could be "as apples of gold," and a Scripture passage included in correspondence may encourage someone many miles away.

As your knowledge of Scripture increases, you may find ever-widening doors open to you. Through memorizing the Word of God, you will be training yourself to become "an instrument for noble purposes, made holy, useful to the Master and prepared to do any good work" (2 Tim. 2:21).

## The Time to Begin Is Now!

As you've read through this chapter, you've seen how the Lord uses people in various walks of life and under various circumstances who have memorized his Word. Perhaps you have said to yourself, "I wish I could memorize Scripture too, but I am too busy" (or "I have no time" or "I am not able"). Before you decide that memorizing God's Word is something you cannot do, remember what Charles Swindoll said, "No other practice in the Christian life is more rewarding, practically speaking, than memorizing Scripture." And the greatest authority of all, the Spirit of truth, declares through the psalmist that the Scriptures

are more precious than gold,
    than much pure gold;
they are sweeter than honey,
    than honey from the comb (Psa. 19:10).

Do you desire to become rich in the things that count, not only for time but also for eternity? Then invest your time and energy in what will bring the greatest reward. Decide *now* to memorize Scripture. Don't put it off. Don't wait till next week, or next month, or some later date. Begin today! Buy a pack of three-by-five cards, fill them with the verses you want to learn, and begin reading them repeatedly every day. Carry through in the strength the Lord will give as you depend on him. Master the verses systematically, and then persist in your reviews regularly. You will never regret it. You too will find God's words of truth to be "more precious than gold."

## CrossCheck

1. Charles Swindoll says, "No other single practice in the Christian life is more rewarding, practically speaking, than memorizing Scripture." What might be some of the rewards he has in mind?

2. Which of the several benefits of memorizing Scripture do you find the most motivating for your own efforts at Scripture memory?

3. Have you, like the author of this chapter, been frustrated by failed attempts at memorizing Scripture? How might the card system he recommends increase your chances of success?

4. Select several verses you've always wanted to memorize and write them on three-by-five cards. For the next thirty days, use the card system described in this chapter, then evaluate its effectiveness.

**James Braga** has been a missionary to China, a pastor, and for many years a professor and chaplain at Multnomah Bible College in Portland, Oregon. He is the author of *How to Prepare Bible Messages* and *How to Study the Bible.*

CHAPTER 3

# Prayer

### *David C. Needham*

**T**he possibility of making a complete mess of one's Christian life and witness haunts many of God's people. And always at the root of spiritual shipwreck is weakness in one's prayer life. Though we all agree that prayer is a wonderful privilege God has given us and we all should do it more, we do it less. To talk to God sounds like such an easy thing to do, yet most of us find it not easy at all. We try to have effective times in prayer. We try and fail and then try again. How many times do you try before you finally decide it's a lost cause?

## Why Is Prayer So Difficult?

Maybe you don't find prayer difficult at all. You pray regularly and it's never a struggle. You enjoy it every time. If that describes your prayer life, wonderful! I hope it never changes.

But I have not found it to be that way. Sometimes I've found prayer easy; at other times it's most difficult. In the first twenty or so years of my Christian life, I found prayer so difficult that I avoided it at every opportunity. Oh, I made promises to God that I would spend time every day talking to him in prayer, and for a while I did. But when I prayed, my mind would wander, and I would think of a dozen other things. God seemed so far away. Then I'd read some verses and call it quits. Well, I'd tell myself, maybe next time it will be better. But "next time" usually meant a week or so later. This pattern went on year after year.

Not that prayer is now easy for me, because it isn't. I still struggle. But over the years God has taught me a few lessons about why it's hard to pray, and he's given me some answers as to what to do about it.

## Prayer is so mysterious

We need to realize that *praying to our God is a mysterious thing.* Think about it. When I pray, I'm talking to somebody I can't see. Not only that, but he's not going to talk back, at least not in the normal sense. God can speak any time he wants and in an audible voice if he chooses. He has in the past and I imagine he will again, but he hasn't yet spoken out loud to me. That makes for a strange conversation.

Not only that, when I pray I am talking to the supreme ruler of the universe. Here I am, this tiny speck on this tiny speck of a planet in a galaxy that's a speck in the universe. And I'm going to address the one who directs the whole show? That's hard to fathom. And at the same moment I'm talking to him, countless other prayers are ascending to his throne. Mine is just one among thousands, probably millions.

And I begin to think, what difference does it make? Does my prayer mean anything to God? Can he respond to me, or is he preoccupied with so much else that I have just a flicker of his attention, as though for just a moment he glances my way and then he must attend to that multitude of other requests?

Many years ago I was a pastor in a little church in southern California, and the people in that church were dear Christian people. They loved me and I loved them, yet I felt discouraged. One night I was so troubled that I got out of bed, got dressed, and walked down the hillside to the ocean.

It was dark except for a big moon hanging over the ocean. I felt so small, so weak, and God seemed so far away. Then I looked at the moon and for a moment forgot about myself. Not only was the moon a majestic sight, but it cast a streak of light all the way across the ocean, all the way up to my feet. On either side of that bright streak the ocean was dark, but there to my feet it was light. It was as though all the light of the moon was coming toward me. I took a step to the right, and the light from the moon followed me. I ran along the sand and looked at the moon as I ran, and the light followed me all the way, always directly to me. When I stopped, it stopped. When I moved, it moved with me.

I thought, *David, the moon is putting on a show just for you!* Then I thought, *What if there were thousands of people along the beach, would each of them see a personal display of the glory of the moon?* And I concluded, yes, they would, and each display would be distinct and personalized.

Then God gave me the grace to make a simple adjustment and remind myself, *David, that's the way God is.* God can shine toward every human being who turns his or her face toward God. The tragedy is that most people have their back toward God. God is shining toward everyone, and yet, because of the kind of being he is, his total attention is directed my way. In the mystery of mysteries, God can give all of his attention to me and at the same time give all of his attention to somebody else. What a God!

One of the reasons prayer is hard is we don't think about the wonder of what's really happening. Just think of it—when I talk to God, I have his attention. All that he is, is directed my way. I urge you in your praying, think about what's going on. Think about what you're going to be doing when you talk to God. What an amazing thing prayer is.

## I don't feel worthy

There's another reason I find prayer hard. *I don't feel worthy to talk to God.* Perhaps I've been so busy with other things, I've neglected time with God, and I imagine he's disappointed in me. It's hard to talk with someone who's disappointed in you. The Bible tells me that I can grieve the Holy Spirit. God does indeed get sad about me, so there may be times when I'm not kidding myself when I think he must not be pleased with me.

What do you say to a God you've just disappointed? What do you do in prayer when you've failed him? The standard answer is that you confess your sins. I haven't found that too hard to do, have you? "Lord, I blew it again. I'm sorry. Lord, when will I ever learn?" I don't find it hard to agree with God that my life is not the way it ought to be.

But does confession of sin make me feel comfortable with God? Normally it doesn't. Yes, I know I'm forgiven, but I still disappointed him. Why did I hurt the one who loves me? I can accept forgiveness with one hand and still hold in my other hand all the feelings of unpleasantness and sadness because of my failure. Confession in itself has not smoothed things out so that I can now smile and look up to God and say, "God, isn't it wonderful we have such good fellowship together." No, I disappointed him. I'm forgiven, but I'm not yet comfortable in his presence.

How do I get comfortable with God if confession doesn't do it? Some people would say I have to get my life straightened around first, and there's some truth to that. There are some things I can do. If there's a barrier between me and another brother or sister, Jesus says I need to seek reconciliation (Matt. 5:23-24). But if I can't have fellowship with God until I have all of my sin problems worked out, that means I have to work them out by myself. I can't do that. In fact, *when I'm sinning is when I need God the most.*

Sometimes when we make these classic doctrinal statements—"Sin breaks fellowship with God"—we create for God's people problems that God never intended. I have found some of my choicest times of fellowship with God are when I am struggling with a sin. I need to talk to him about it—"Lord, you know about my problem. You also know the way out. Lord, please help me." As long as I want to please God, fellowship is there even though the sin problem hasn't disappeared. Any loving father whose son comes to him and says, "Daddy, I know you don't want me to lie, but I do it without thinking and I'm sorry. Please help me," would say. "Okay, son, let's talk about it. Let's see if we can understand why you sometimes have a hard time telling the truth."

If prayer has been hard for you because you've felt you're

just not fit to talk to God, then realize this: his love and his grace have opened wide the door to fellowship right in the middle of your struggles. The Lord reaches out to me, not when I have everything all worked out but when I don't. The only thing he asks of me is that I really want him—that's all.

But still I struggle. All too often when I pray, I think about my failures, my weaknesses, and they become a weight on my shoulders. During such low times in prayer, I need to remind myself, *David, focus on God. Start thinking about what kind of God he is. He's a God of awesome power who rules the universe. David, look at the stars. He put all that up there and he upholds it there by the word of his power. Oh, what a God!* And I find my head's lifted up, and I'm no longer thinking about myself. I become lost in thinking about him.

## Do my prayers really make a difference?

I also find prayer difficult because *it's so hard for me to believe that my prayers make any difference.* I've prayed and it doesn't seem to have made any difference, and so I conclude maybe it doesn't. Maybe the only reason I should pray is because prayer changes me. But does the Bible say that's the only reason I should pray? Does my prayer change what God will do? My Bible says *yes!*

- You do not have, because you do not ask God (Js. 4:2).
- "Ask and you will receive" (John 16:24).
- "You may ask me for anything in my name, and I will do it" (John 14:14).
- The prayer of a righteous man is powerful and effective (Js. 5:16).

The Bible says my prayers affect what God does. Since God says it is so, then I must believe him. But why should my prayers affect what God does? He's a God of infinite wisdom, infinite power, tremendous purposes. Why would he ever hold back doing something waiting for me to pray?

About the time I entered high school, my dad decided to plant some more avocado trees on the ranch where we lived, and he said, "Son, how would you like that acreage of avocado trees to be your responsibility, everything from the first planting right on through?" I felt good that my dad trusted me with such a big responsibility, and so I said, "That would be great, Dad." Soon I was on a tractor preparing the hillside. Then I ordered and planted the trees and plowed long furrows for irrigation. They were my responsibility.

The following summer, I noticed that some of the trees at the ends of the rows were looking a bit wilted, so I made sure the water got all of the way through to the last tree. When I irrigated the trees again a few weeks later, I discovered they were no better—in fact, the tips of some of the leaves were brittle. So I sprinkled some fertilizer around them and hoped that would take care of it. I checked the trees again a few weeks later and some looked as though they were going to die. At last I went to my dad and said, "Dad, you know those trees that have been my responsibility? Some of them look like they're not going to make it."

And my dad said, "Yes, son, I've been watching them. I think some of them are going to die." "You knew about it?" "Yes, and I know what will make them grow again." "All these weeks those trees were suffering and you knew what to do and you didn't tell me? Why, Dad?"

"Son, I wanted to see developed in you a farmer's heart. I wanted you to feel the way I feel, and I was willing to wait until you came. Now that you've come, I'll tell you what we need to do." Then he told me of a layer of clay just a few inches under the surface that kept the water from penetrating; he knew of a way to break through it so the water could get to the trees' roots. He knew what to do, but he waited until I came to him because he wanted me to share his heart.

Paul says we are fellow workers with God (1 Cor. 3:9). Isn't that an amazing thought? One of the reasons God will hold back from doing something until I come to him is because he wants me to be a coworker with him, to share his heart, his concern. Sometimes it takes a while for me to come in line with the heart of God. When I finally do, God answers. Yes, there is a reason why God waits for my prayers.

But I could still say, "Doesn't the Bible teach that God has ordained all things before the foundation of the world? If, in the infinite, eternal mind of God, everything is programmed, how can my praying change what is going to happen?"

This is one of the great mysteries. The Bible clearly teaches the absolute sovereign purposes of God, yet the Bible also says that my praying changes what God would otherwise have done. I wonder if those two truths are somehow brought together in the mystery of God being eternal. Even though he is eternal, he normally chooses to move through time with us. Our future is future to him too. But he doesn't need to do this. He can see all of time as one indivisible present. From a moment in time my prayer ascends to God, but he may choose to hear it in that mysterious eternal moment when he solidifies all of his purposes for all of time.

When I come before the throne of grace, before my infinite God, I see myself pausing at the door of his eternal council chamber. He beckons me to enter, and I say, "Father, I have a request. Would you please so fill me with your power that Jesus might be seen through me more perfectly?" And the Father says to me, "David, that is exactly what I would like to see. We'll put that in my eternal purposes." And he does...in answer to my prayer.

What a mystery prayer is. When you pray, God acts; if you don't pray, he may not act. My prayer actually moves the hand of God.

## My mind keeps wandering

I have found prayer difficult at times because *I find it hard to concentrate.* I start off just fine, and then I realize I've been thinking about what I ate for breakfast, or some other insignificant thing. My thoughts have had no connection with God and prayer, and it's discouraging.

One of our problems, if we've been Christians for a while, is we've discovered how to pray without thinking. We've become experts at it. We have a bunch of little phrases that sound good, and we use them without thinking. My mind can be somewhere else, yet I can easily say, "Lord Jesus, thank you for dying on the cross for my sin." They're words already programmed into my brain.

We must learn to be tough on ourselves, to force ourselves to think when we pray. When you find yourself saying something like, "Dear heavenly Father, thank you that you love me," don't say anything more. Stop and ask the Lord, "What does it mean that you love me? Oh, Holy Spirit, teach me what it means." Spend time meditating on what the Bible says about God's love for you, and then thank him for his great love. We are too flippant in our prayers. We need to think *hard* when we pray.

In addition, we often begin our prayers by thanking God for this and asking him for that and interceding for so-and-so, but we haven't stopped to focus on where our prayers are going and what's involved in prayer. Think of some of the significant prayers in the New Testament, such as the Lord's prayer, which begins, "Our Father in heaven..." You may think, *What an unnecessary thing to say. Everybody knows he's in heaven. Why say it?* Jesus didn't consider it unnecessary, a waste of words. When we pray, "Our Father," we should stop and picture God *in heaven,* surrounded by myriads of angels. As I pray out of my smallness and my difficulties, my pain and my loneliness, where does my prayer take me? To my Father *in heaven,* enthroned and shining forth with all the radiance of his glory. Picture in your mind the "holy, holy, holy" echoing through the ramparts of heaven, as Isaiah describes it in Isaiah 6. See yourself walking into the throne room of God, surrounded by the anthem of the angels, and with your tiny voice speaking to this infinite Lord...and he says, "I'm listening."

If you find your mind wandering when you pray, spend a few moments getting focused. Don't immediately begin making requests or confessing your sins; think about what's happening. Where is my prayer ascending? What is God like? What are his resources? How does he feel about me?

Then bring your requests.

Here's another tip to help you keep your mind from wandering. I've found that it helps me to pray out loud and, if it's comfortable to do so, to pray with my eyes open. Sometimes keeping my eyes open helps me to remember, "God's here."

Another practice that's helped me concentrate is to walk when I pray. I take a walk with God. I go out when it's getting dark and most people are in their houses (or at least they're not watching me), and I walk and talk to God.

I've also found it difficult to concentrate when others lead in prayer. I hate to admit it, but all too often I analyze their prayer instead of praying with them. When they say, "Amen," I suddenly wake up to the fact that I haven't prayed at all. It's helped me to realize that when someone else is praying, I don't have to think about what to say—they're doing that for me—so that frees me to concentrate on what is being said. Often I picture myself walking with the person who is praying into the throne room of God, and up above is the Father on his throne with the Lord Jesus by his side. The person I'm with is the spokesman, and I'm standing by and saying, "That's right. Thank you, Lord, for hearing what he's saying." I can enjoy the sheer pleasure of communication without having to create the words. But I have to consciously do that, otherwise I become just an analyzer and an evaluator, which is inexcusable. Be tough on yourself. Think when you are praying

Finally, if you spend half an hour talking to the Lord and suddenly realize you've been daydreaming and have spent only five minutes praying, then rather than be depressed about the twenty-five minutes you wasted, remember the five minutes you didn't. Value the times of genuine prayer, and trust those times will get longer as you become more disciplined in prayer. Don't berate yourself for the wasted time. The Lord values even those few minutes when we're really praying.

## Prayer seems too good to be true

Another reason prayer is hard is that it *seems too good to be true*. Look at these promises from Jesus:

> "Ask and it will be given to you; seek and you will find; knock and the door will be opened to you. For everyone who asks receives; he who seeks finds; and to him who knocks, the door will be opened" (Matt. 7: 7-8).

> "I tell you the truth, if you have faith and do not doubt, not only can you do what was done to the fig tree, but also you can say to this mountain, 'Go, throw yourself into the sea,' and it will be done. If you believe, you will receive whatever you ask for in prayer" (Matt. 21:21-22).

After reading these verses you may think, "Anything I ask for I'm going to get? Fantastic!" If that's your attitude, *watch out*. If you're not careful, God will become to you nothing more than a genie in a bottle, a magic stone you rub and say, "Here's what I want"—and God does it. Isn't that what the Bible says? If you want to be rich, believe it and you will. If you want to be healthy, just believe it and you will.

Is that what this business of prayer is all about, asking and getting? Is the key to prayer believing that I will get what I've asked for so that if I believe hard enough, God becomes obligated to snap to and do it? Is that Christianity?

That's what some popular teachers would have us believe. But what a mockery that is of the whole message of the Word of God. Christianity is not a means to get what I want. Above all else, it is a love relationship between my Savior and me. God will not be my genie, he will not be my slave. He is always Lord, and I come and make my requests before him, acknowledging that he alone is Wisdom, he alone knows best.

Remember, before you latch onto a verse in the Bible, be sure that it blends with all that the Scriptures say. The Bible also says this about prayer:

This is the confidence we have in approaching God: that if we ask anything *according to his will,* he hears us. And if we know that he hears us—whatever we ask—we know that we have what we asked of him (1 John 5:14-15).

To have any assurance that our prayers will be answered, we need to be sure we are asking according to God's will, not merely according to our desires. In John 14 and 15, Jesus says in various ways, "If you ask anything in my name, I will do it." If we ask anything in harmony with Jesus' name—anything he would approve—he will do it.

My relationship with Jesus is a love relationship where I come to know him, his mind and his will. How do I know his will? I come to know the truth of God, the mind of God, the will of God as I fill my thoughts with the truth of his Word. Then I can know what is the good, pleasing, and perfect will of God, and then I will know what to ask from him (Rom. 12:2). If I think of prayer as simply a magic potion, then I've missed the whole purpose God saved me for.

I am so glad God doesn't answer all of my prayers. I can think of some prayers that if he'd answered them, it would have been tragic. In a Bible I had when I was in high school, I wrote a phone number in the margin of Psalm 37, right next to the verses that say: "Delight thyself also in the LORD; and he shall give thee the desires of thine heart. Commit thy way unto the LORD; trust also in him; and he shall bring it to pass" (KJV).

The phone number was that of a girl I wanted to be mine for the rest of my life—or at least for the rest of the year. One of the kindest things God ever did was to not "bring it to pass." You say, "But wasn't she the desire of your heart?" I guess she was in a shallow way, but God knew the desires of my heart went far deeper than Billie Ann. He knew to give me that shallow answer would be to frustrate the deepest desire of my heart, which was God himself. He knows the desires of our heart better than we do...and I'm glad he does.

## But I don't feel anything

Another reason I find prayer difficult is that *so often the feelings I want to feel aren't there.* Sometimes when I talk to God, I enjoy a sense of intimacy and of delight in him. When I don't experience those feelings, I assume something must be wrong. That isn't necessarily so. You and I can't possibly live on an emotional high all the time. We're just not built to handle such constant emotional intensity.

Sometimes in prayer I become more conscious of how I'm feeling than of who I'm talking to. It's like going to a basketball game and spending my time thinking, *How am I reacting to the game? Should I get a little more excited? Come on, David, show some excitement!* The moment I become so self-conscious, I cannot get excited at all. The same is true in prayer—the moment I become self-conscious, I frustrate any feelings of intimacy and enjoyment of God. I need to learn to walk by faith and not by sight...or by feelings.

Even if I'm not self-conscious, I still may not always experience the presence of God. Sometimes when I talk to God and I feel emotionally down, that can be due to nothing more than an underactive thyroid or not enough sleep—there's no spiritual basis for it at all. Yet I too readily think it must be a spiritual problem. And so I need to ask myself, *David, is there any barrier between you and God that you haven't dealt with?* No, I don't think so. *As far as you know everything is all right?* Yes. *Then David, affirm God's love apart from feelings.* Isn't that a little hypocritical? *Not a bit, because it's true. He does love me whether I feel it or not.*

At times I have been so aware of my lack of emotional response to God that I've wondered what the angels, who are always praising God, must think. When that occurs, I sometimes feel I need to say to them, "Listen, all principalities and powers, all righteous angels and all evil angels. I exalt my God and I affirm his love. Even though at this moment I don't feel it, I'm committed to him, I belong to him. He is my Lord. You have no right to question my relationship to him."

Be careful with seeking feelings. Instead, talk to God

about how great he is, recounting what the Bible says about him. We need to mull over the kind of God he is, not focusing on ourselves, just focusing on him.

## God is so different from me

Sometimes I've found prayer difficult because *it's hard to talk to someone who's so different from me.* God is so different. He's the Lord of the universe, and I'm just an insignificant little speck. He's perfect and holy, and I'm such a sinner. Forgiven, yes, but what a worm I am. What do God and I have in common?

The most exciting discovery I've made since I was saved as a child is that when I was born again, God performed a miracle so big that he and I *do* have things in common. The moment I was born again, I was not only forgiven, but God *changed* me. The moment you are saved, the core of who you are changes from flesh to spirit. You are now a new creation, a partaker of the divine nature (2 Pet. 1:4).

When I talk to God, I don't come to someone who is of a different nature than I am. He will always be God and I will always be his subject; I will never become part of God. Nevertheless, the very nature of God has been given to me. Christ lives in me. I am now his workmanship. I am now a child of God, dead to sin and alive to God because in my inner being I delight in God's law. I am a new creation.

When I go out to pray at night, I'm humbled before the majesty of God, and sometimes I'm hesitant to warm up to him because I start thinking of how different he is from me. And then, amazement of amazement, I start thinking, *Wait a minute, David. You and God have something in common. Your heart of hearts beats with his heart. He loves holiness and deep inside, you love holiness too. He is light. You are a child of the light; you are not in darkness. Heaven is the place of his glory and heaven is your home, the place of your citizenship.* And I marvel at the miracle of God's grace and at the power of the new birth.

### Taste and See

It is wonderful to know that God "has qualified you to share in the inheritance of the saints in the kingdom of light" (Col. 1:12). Heaven is your destiny. But God had something even more precious in mind when he saved you. He saved you for himself; he seeks intimacy. And at the heart of that intimacy is prayer.

On our ranch in southern California we also grew lemons, oranges, and alfalfa—crops you know something about. But you probably don't know anything about another crop we grew, a subtropical fruit called cherimoya. Now I could describe cherimoya to you—I could tell you what it looks like, the kind of seeds it has, whether it's sour or sweet, juicy or dry. I could even tell you how many vitamins, minerals, and calories are in it. Would you know what a cherimoya is? Not really. To know what a cherimoya is you need to see one and, better yet, taste it.

That's why I like so well the Bible's beautiful invitation, "Taste and see that the LORD is good" (Psa. 34:8). God desires that our knowledge of him be based not primarily upon so many facts we memorize, but upon a love relationship where we taste and experience what our God is like.

We worship a mysterious God, a God who fills heaven and earth. Yet though he is everywhere, he is primarily a God who seeks relationships. He is a mysterious God, but he's also a person, a real person we can talk to. Because I am his child, his presence—literally, "his face"—is my way. Becoming a Christian is not just believing certain bits of information; it is receiving a person (John 1:12). The gospel, the message of reconciliation, is that God and I have become friends. When I bow before him and talk to him, his face is my way—he's looking right at me. That's the essence of prayer.

When our son was six years old, he attended an elementary school just below where our house is located on the side of a hill. We can see the playground from the windows in our living room, and a number of times during the day my wife, Mary Jo, would go to those windows and see if she could spot Greg running around at recess with all those hundreds of little bodies. Sometimes she would notice a little hand go up and wave toward home. Greg couldn't see her in the window, but he figured Mommy's face was his way. And Mary Jo said, "I wonder how many times he's waved and I didn't see him."

Isn't it a wonderful thing, when we come before God and "wave," his face is always our way—*always*. And even when we're not praying, his face is still our way, because he has promised that he will never leave us. The ultimate tragedy for a human being is to come to the end of his life having rejected the heart-longing of God for his soul, and then by a sovereign edict of God, for that person to go into eternal darkness where God will never look his way again, forever away from the face of God.

Confessing, asking, interceding, thanking—all are fitting aspects of prayer. But the heart of prayer goes deeper. God's face is my way. I see him. I know him. He invites me to draw near...and I do. I stand on tiptoes, stretching fingers skyward. I speak in whispers, drinking in acceptance, almost forgetting to breathe. He loves me! God loves me. And we talk.

## CrossCheck

1. Do you agree or disagree with the statement, "Always at the root of spiritual shipwreck is weakness in one's prayer life"? If you agree, why do you think this is so?

2. The author gives several reasons why prayer is difficult. Which reasons best describe your own struggles with prayer?

3. Rate your prayer life on a scale of 1 to 10 (1 being "nonexistent" and 10 being "without ceasing"). What changes in attitude or practice would you need to make to move your score one number higher?

4. Think about the reality that God's face is always your way. How might that knowledge affect your praying?

**David C. Needham** has taught Bible and theology for more than twenty-five years at Multnomah Bible College in Portland, Oregon. He is the author of *Birthright: Christian, Do You Know Who You Are?* and *Close to His Majesty: An Invitation to Walk with God.*

# CHAPTER 4

# Worship

*Ronald B. Allen*

*A funny thing happened on the way to church one Sunday. A family determined they were going to practice the discipline of the worship of the living God.*

A *funny* thing? Perhaps it was more of an unusual thing. But it need not remain unusual. We dare not let it remain so. And certainly not a *funny* thing. But what is this thing? What do we mean by the discipline of the worship of God?

## Rediscovering the Missing Jewel

The subject of worship is an area of controversy among Christians. More than a decade ago, Gordon Borror, professor of church music at Western Seminary in Portland, Oregon, and I wrote a book on biblical worship for evangelical churches. A few disturbing things happened when our book, *Worship: Rediscovering the Missing Jewel*, began to "get around." One manager of a Christian bookstore in the Midwest was ordered by his superior to return all copies of our book (as well as other titles by the same publisher). The reason? A book on worship was a part of liberalism in the church.

Liberalism! How in the world could that association be made with worship? It is astonishing to me, but that association has been made by a number of people.

The reason seems to lie in the fact that in many of the mainline denominations, there has been a strong interest in the renewal of worship. Since these churches are no longer

Bible-teaching churches, an interest in worship must come at the cost of an emphasis on the teaching of the Word of God.

More than one of the great Bible preachers whose names are well-known in evangelical circles has spoken against an emphasis on worship. Some regard music with suspicion. Some feel that an interest in worship may detract from their time for preaching. Some have said that worship is something people may do in their private lives, but when they come to church it is to hear the Word of God.

But the preaching of the Word of God and the worship of the Person of God are handmaidens, not bickering sisters. When preaching is what it ought to be, worship will be the natural outcome. When worship is what it ought to be, preaching will be more important than ever. We may need to add a few more minutes to our services to do all things well, but we need not curtail biblical preaching in order to practice biblical worship.

But things are changing, even in conservative circles. Pastors and laity alike are responding to the need for a renewal of worship in all of our churches. Worship is finally being recognized among biblical people as a biblical issue—something of great importance for people of faith in God.

Worship is being rediscovered. Worship is coming into its own in our lives. This is the work, we believe, of God's Spirit. And we welcome the change.

But what is biblical worship? *True worship is the people's grateful response to the living God, done according to his commands, each from a free and willing heart, seeking to bring glory to his Person.*

## A Rose by Any Other Name?

Have you ever reflected on some of the ways Christian denominations describe themselves? Some churches honor their spiritual founders (Lutheran, Wesleyan). Other churches are named for their manner of organization and government (Episcopal, Congregational). Some churches are named for practices or distinctive beliefs they hold as very important (Baptist, Pentecostal). Some church names seem to imply that they offer what one may not get in another type of church. (Does the name "Bible" church imply the Bible may not be taken as seriously elsewhere?) Many churches in our country are ethnic, while other churches have sought in their names to minimize distinctions (or to make them less prominent).

Among all these varied names, *how few speak of the manner of worship.* We have named our churches for nearly everything associated with our faith except for the worship of God. Is this because we have not given it sufficient thought? Is it because worship is not sufficiently valued?

How can it be that worship is not valued by churches which cherish the Scripture, which adhere to sound doctrine, where God is loved, where Christ is honored, and where the Spirit is heard? Surely this is a sin of omission. This cannot be a pathway we deliberately chose.

A few years ago I ministered for several days in a church in New Hampshire—quite a distance from my Oregon home. My host, in a gesture of friendship, said he had once lived in the West. I asked him where. He replied in all seriousness, "I lived for a couple of years in Western Pennsylvania. But I didn't like it, so I moved back home."

I suppose if one has lived all his life in New England, the western wilderness of Pennsylvania somehow merges into vistas of the Pacific. And if one has gone to church all one's life without much thought of worship, there may be a similar sense of strangeness, and dislike, when people begin to discuss it.

## As Go the Seminaries, So Go the Churches

I went to a splendid theological seminary for my training in Christian ministry. I am still a grateful alumnus of my school. We were taught well in biblical studies, in theology, and in biblical languages. We had wonderful courses in evangelism, in pastoral ministry, and in the art of sermon preparation. We had solid courses in Christian education and world mission. We even had some work in counseling and in small groups.

But there was one area in which we had no training at all. In my four years of full-time studies for my Master of Theology degree, there was no requirement at all in the study of biblical worship. It is not that I missed that course or did not like a certain professor. There was no course—no required course, no elective course, not even a lecture.

Think about that. Is this not like saying to a lawyer, "Were you asleep on the day they taught law in law school?" How could one go to seminary and not be taught to lead in the worship of God?

We had the most solid, practical, and relevant preparation for Christian ministry that could be received anywhere at the time, we believed. But there was no training in how to lead people in the worship of God. Nor were we trained to worship him in our own lives.

Now, please understand. We were taught how to pray and were encouraged to pray well and much. We were taught how to read and study the Word of God. We were taught how to baptize, marry, and bury folks. And we were taught to preach. But we were not taught to worship. How then—how in the world, then—could we teach others?

### The Bible: A Book of Worship

In a sense, the Bible is a book of worship. I do not intend to reduce the Bible to one subject, not even to the subject of worship. But worship is a theme that permeates the Scriptures.

After the stories of creation and the Fall, the Bible speaks of the worship of God in the lives of the first family. This is in Genesis 4, the story of Cain and Abel. Yet through history there has likely been more interest shown in the fratricide than in the worship issue that serves as the basis for the story.

But it was an issue of worship. Yahweh looked with satisfaction on the person of Abel and on the offering he presented. Yahweh did not look with satisfaction on the person of Cain nor on what he presented.

The text is brief, but pointed. When Abel presented his offering, the descriptive words indicate that he offered the best he had to the Lord, Yahweh. When Cain presented his offering, there are no descriptive words used. If you are a gardener, you will appreciate this. I think Cain gave the Lord some zucchini! He brought something he had in abundance, without much thought to his attitude or actions.

The text of Genesis 4 states that God looked first at the person, and then at the offering. It was Abel, and then his offering, that Yahweh viewed with satisfaction. It was Cain, and then his offering, that the Lord did not find satisfying.

Genesis 4 sets the stage for our understanding of true worship throughout biblical history. This teaching regarding *the attitudes and desires of the heart* is carried on throughout Scripture (see Micah 6:6-8; Psa. 40:6-8; Rev. 7:9-17).

*True worship is the people's grateful response to the living God, done according to his commands, each from a free and willing heart, seeking to bring glory to his Person.*

If the first story of the Bible following the Fall deals with worship, one of the last accounts in the Old Testament also centers on worship. This is the wonderful account of the great revival under Ezra among the people of the restoration community, described in Nehemiah 8 and 9. (If the Old Testament were arranged chronologically, the Book of Nehemiah would be the last book of the Old Testament.) These chapters in the Book of Nehemiah describe one of the great worship events in the biblical story.

Nehemiah 9 is arguably one of the most significant chapters in the Bible. It is the basic story of the Old Testament expressed in a wonderful psalm. This magnificent chapter begins with an ascription of blessing to the glorious name of the Lord, Yahweh (vv. 5-6). Second, the longer part of the psalm (vv. 7-31) contrasts the unending faithfulness of the Lord and the checkered history of his people. The third section (vv. 32-35) states the present situation of the restoration community as they reflect on their history and consider still the faithfulness of God in their lives. Finally (vv. 36-38), the people turn in full seriousness to the Lord in solemn covenant, promising faithfulness that will be commensurate with God's faithfulness in their lives.

What a text this is! How wonderfully it speaks of the name of God:

> "Stand up and bless the LORD your God
> Forever and ever!

> "Blessed be Your glorious name,
> Which is exalted above all blessing and praise! (9:5).

How wondrously it speaks of the person of God:

> "But You are God,
> Ready to pardon,
> Gracious and merciful,
> Slow to anger,
> Abundant in kindness,
> And did not forsake them" (9:17).

How frankly it confesses sin:

> But they and our fathers acted proudly,
> Hardened their necks,
> And did not heed Your commandments" (9:16).

How strongly it affirms faith and confidence:

> "And because of all this,
> We make a sure covenant, and write it;
> And our leaders and our Levites and our priests seal
>     it" (9:38).

This is a text of glorious corporate worship of God.

Throughout the Old Testament there is a constant emphasis on the true worship of the living God. True biblical worship is often contrasted with two evils: the debasing worship of the gods of the nations (often associated with sexual perversion and inhumane actions); and the improper worship of the living God (done by people with impure motives or by those lacking understanding of the holiness of God).

*True worship is the people's grateful response to the living God, done according to his commands, each from a free and willing heart, seeking to bring glory to his Person.*

The Book of Psalms is entirely a book that centers on the worship of God. The Torah, the first five books of the Bible, has long sections that describe and command true worship, and includes lengthy sections warning against false worship. The Book of Leviticus in its entirety deals with the worship of God. The prophets speak at length on worship, pressing for true worship and condemning false worship of all kinds.

Similarly, there are instances of true worship that help to begin the story-line of the New Testament, and instances of true worship that conclude the pages of the New Testament. Luke's Gospel, for instance, begins with the announcement of the impending conception of John the Baptist. The announcement came to a priest at work in the worship of the Lord (Luke 1:5-25). Mary's visit with her cousin Elizabeth led to their joint worship of God in celebrative song of praise (1:39-56). Zacharias, the priest and the father of John, also led in worship by a song of praise (1:67-79). When the Savior was born, all heaven worshiped (2:13-14); and so did some shepherds (2:20). When the infant Savior was presented in the Temple as an act of worship by his parents (2:21-24), he was greeted by Simeon, a worshiping man powerfully marked by the Holy Spirit (2:25-35). He was also welcomed by Anna, a worshiping prophetess who had been waiting for him (2:36-38).

Again and again in the Gospels and in the Epistles there are teachings on worship and encouragements to continue to worship God in spirit and in truth (see John 4). Much of the Book of Hebrews concerns the worship of God. Songs of praise are found even in the dark, difficult pages of the Book of the Revelation.

Worship is a theme found at the beginning and the conclusion of both Testaments. It is one of the most pervasive themes in Scripture. Entire books of the Bible are given to worship.

### Sacrifice...

Worship in the period of the Hebrew Scriptures was centered on sacrifice. Sacrifices included grains and produce as well as animals, wine as well as lambs, oil and incense as well as rams. Sacrifices were somber times of reflection, of mourning, of fasting, of confession of sins and release of guilt. But sacrifices were also times of feasting and great joy—times of enjoying God and enjoying being his people.

Each of the sacrifices that was done in faith and according to the command of the living God had a meaning beyond itself. In a variety of ways, each of the legitimate sacrifices found its fulfillment in the life, death, and resurrection of the Savior Jesus. Every waving of sheaves of grain was an acknowledgment that all good gifts come from the Father above. Every burning of incense or lighting of candles spoke of realities of heaven that impinge on daily living. Every libation of wine on the altar was a picture of Jesus' life poured out for others. Every whole burned offering was a symbol of his life that was destroyed because of our sin. Each of the communal offerings was a portrait of true fellowship of the redeemed, which comes only through Jesus' death and resurrection.

For this reason, the Christian who reads of sacrifice in the pages of the Old Testament finds his or her thoughts driven to the cross, to the tomb, to the resurrection—and to the communion table.

Evangelical churches are rediscovering the sublime holiness of the celebration of the Lord's table. No longer will we be satisfied to have the Lord's table "tacked-on" and rushed through at the end of a service. Rather, we will make much of the Lord's table. We will observe it sometimes with humbleness, with a sense of pain, and with sorrow. We will observe it sometimes with contemplation, silence, and reflection. We will observe it other times with joy, with brightness, and exuberance.

When we come to the Lord's table we confront the horror of human sinfulness. When we come to the Lord's table we are reminded of the wonder of God's provision. When we come to the Lord's table we are provoked by the sublimity of victory, of battle won, of glory to come.

It is the practice in my church to celebrate the Lord's table on the first Sunday of the month. On those days, the services are special, marked out from others. The entire service is centered on the Lord's Table. We do it different ways. We do it the same way. We do it with prayer, with planning, and with purpose. And we worship the living Christ together.

## ...and Song

Worship in the period of the Hebrew Scriptures was not just about sacrifice; it was also bathed in song. I suspect most Christians think of blood when they think of worship in Old Testament times, and when they think of blood it is with a sense of distaste and distance.

Well, there was blood. At times there must have been great amounts of blood. The conditions were not pleasant. The blood of sacrifices would be associated with bleating animals, hot sun, flies, and stench.

But when the righteous came to worship the living God, they did not come with apprehension or distaste. They came with joy. This is what they sang to one another:

Make a joyful shout to the LORD, all you lands!
Serve the LORD with gladness;
Come before His presence with singing (Psa. 100:1-2).

They came with song because they came with joy. As important as blood was in some of the sacrifices in biblical worship, music was also paramount. Music was the means of expressing joy in knowing the living God. Music was the means of demonstrating oneness among his people. Music was the means of stating one's hurts and frustrations to the Lord. Music accompanied prayer. Music was the means of praise. Music and the worship of the living God were inseparable.

Gordon Borror says that to be a Christian and not to be a singer is like being a fish and not being a swimmer. By this he does not mean that when one comes to faith one becomes a natural Pavarotti. But he does mean that it is incomprehensible to imagine biblical worship apart from song.

It is so important for song to be made more prominent in our worship services. Music should not be a filler, merely to allow latecomers to find their seats. Music should not be a preliminary, getting people in the mood to hear spiritual things. Music *is* the thing. Biblical worship must make much of music. Worship is more than music, but worship apart from music is greatly impoverished.

Praise the LORD!
For it is good to sing praises to our God;
For it is pleasant, and praise is beautiful
(Psa. 147:1).

## Verb and Noun

Robert Webber rightly insists that *worship* is a verb. That is, worship is an issue of action and activity. It is not something passive or static. Worship is something we do.

Worship is like swimming or bicycling. People who enjoy either activity likely enjoy reading about the activity as well. When I began cycling a few years ago, I discovered several magazines devoted entirely to that activity. I have subscribed to one of these, and I read it each month from cover to cover. I read about new products, about improving technique, about diet, rest, recovery, and about new places to ride and groups to join for rides. But what that magazine does more than anything else is to keep bicycling a verb in my life. The more I read about cycling, the more I want to do it.

The same should be true of worship. We need to read and study about worship. But more, we need to do it.

It is also important to emphasize the *worshiper*. Worship is both a word to describe what we do and a term to indicate who we are. Worshipers worship. When other than true worshipers come to worship the living God, their actions are rejected and their attitudes are judged. This is the clear teaching of the Bible from Genesis to Revelation. Abel was a worshiper; Cain was just a person doing actions of worship. Aaron was a worshiper; in time his sons Nadab and Abihu became abusers of true worship. David was a worshiper, but Saul had become a person who merely brought sacrifices to the Lord.

The priests were supposed to lead in true worship in biblical times. Often they were the ones judged most severely for their acts of irreligion and impiety. The laity sometimes worshiped in the right manner because they were the ones who were right within themselves.

*True worship is the people's grateful response to the living God, done according to his commands, each from a free and willing heart, seeking to bring glory to his Person.*

### Personal and Corporate

The Bible has a great deal to say, of course, about personal worship. It is expected that a person will have an active prayer life, an engaging spiritual vitality based on knowing God, and an ongoing desire to make him known. But the emphasis of Scripture is on worship that we do together. Corporate worship is "where the action is."

The lovely, plaintive words of Psalms 42 and 43 show this to be the case. An exile from Jerusalem found himself to be so deeply pained that he groaned aloud,

As the deer pants for the water brooks,
So pants my soul for You, O God (Psa. 42:1).

He was a worshiper of God. His thoughts were consumed with thoughts of God. He was in prayer to God. He was in song to God. But he was away from the Temple. He was away from the pilgrims who would come to feast and to worship. And he was being destroyed within. He did his best to console his inner being with the hope that one day he would return and praise God in the Temple (see Psa. 42:5, 11; 43:5).

The reason worship is a corporate act is found in what worship does. Worship *does* things for the worshiper, for the community, and for God himself. Worship allows us to express our heart to the living God. While that is a very personal thing, it is not a lonely thing. The individual learns worship in the group. And the group is encouraged and directed by the worship acts of the individuals.

And worship brings new beauty to the Lord. This is stated in one of the great hymns of worship in the Bible, Israel's response to their deliverance from Egypt and the Sea.

> The LORD is my strength and song,
> And He has become my salvation;
> He is my God, and I will praise Him;
> My father's God, and I will exalt Him

(Exod. 15:2).

The words, "I will praise Him," may also be translated, "I will beautify Him." Here is the great mystery. When we worship God in truth, we bring new beauty to his infinite loveliness.

*True worship is the people's grateful response to the living God, done according to his commands, each from a free and willing heart, seeking to bring glory to his Person.*

Years ago, when I was an announcer on an all-classical music station in Dallas, I produced a series of radio spots for a local church. I was really proud of one of the ads in the series. I had taken a few measures from an old vocal recording and a few measures from a Beethoven symphony. In my "voice-over" I said something about some old things being dated, and how other old things were timeless. Then I said, "The Bible is like that. It is very old, much older than the music of Beethoven. But every time it is read with understanding, it is timeless." Then there was the tag that named a church where the Bible could be heard.

When I completed this, I took it to my supervisor at the station and asked her opinion of my work. When she listened, she frowned. Finally, she said, "You have done really good work, but I don't like it. Religion is too personal an issue to talk about in public. You are speaking about the Bible as though it were just another part of life. For me, this is a very private thing." She was not a worshiper. Whatever her faith was, she kept it private as a matter of principle.

But biblical faith is not something held in secret; biblical worship is not something hidden in privacy. Biblical worship is a most public thing. When a person gives great praise to God for an answer to prayer, it is not just the individual who praises God, but the community. The reason we share requests with one another is to involve one another in the praise that will come when the Lord responds to the request.

## With My Voice

Praise is so central to the worship of God in the Psalms that it is difficult to imagine worship apart from the praise of God. To praise God is to make one's boast in him. It is to celebrate him. It is to enjoy him openly, publicly, vocally.

Praise, as the Psalms describe it, is not something done silently or in private. I know that sounds strange to us, because we have become used to speaking of "silent praise" or "private praise." When the psalmists spoke of praise, they had no notion of something to be done in a private, quiet moment. They spoke of sound made in the community:

Praise the LORD!
Sing to the LORD a new song,
And His praise in the congregation of the saints
(Psa. 149:1).

We have not really praised the Lord merely by saying, "Praise the Lord" or "Hallelujah." We have only used the words to encourage one another to be about the business of boasting in his wonder, of sharing his mercies, of saying aloud something about his goodness. The psalmists speak of this as an ongoing vocation in the life of faith:

Praise the LORD!
Praise the LORD O my soul!
While I live I will praise the LORD;
I will sing praises to my God while I have my being
(Psa. 146:1-2).

Our worship of God ought to be better than that done in the period of the Old Testament. Better, because we have even more to celebrate in the finished work of the Savior Jesus. Better, because we have no sacrifices to bring other than the sacrifices of our lips (Heb. 13:15). Better, because we may learn from the mistakes of the past and worship in spirit and truth (John 4:23-24). Better, because we have the completed message in the Word of God. Better, because we are the heirs of the ages (Tit. 3:7). Better for a thousand reasons.

But our worship will not even happen unless we regard it as significant. Our worship will not even happen unless we determine, by the grace of God, and in the power of the Spirit, to be biblical in our worship. Our worship will not even happen unless we plan to do it.

Biblical worship is a discipline of faith. Fish swim. Cyclists cycle. Worshipers worship.

*A wonderful thing happened on the way to church one Sunday. A family determined to worship the living God. And when they participated in word, song, and ceremony, they sensed God's pleasure.*

## CrossCheck

1. Do you agree with the author's definition of biblical worship? What changes, if any, would you make to that definition?

2. The author says that worship is a theme that permeates the Scriptures and cites several examples. Give two or three additional biblical examples where this theme is evident.

3. What place does music play in worship that is biblical?

4. Give some of your reasons why worship today ought to be better than worship during the Old Testament period.

5. Did you worship during last Sunday's "worship service"? If not, what changes do you need to make this Sunday to practice the discipline of the worship of the living God?

**Ronald B. Allen** is professor of Hebrew Scripture at Western Seminary, Portland, Oregon, where he has taught for over twenty years. He is the author of a dozen books and numerous articles and essays.

CHAPTER 5

# Giving

## *Garry Friesen*
### *with J. Robin Maxson*

J esus said, "It is more blessed to give than to receive" (Acts 20:35). For many Christians, however, the joy of giving to the Lord has been blunted by the pressure to give—pressure generated by the sheer volume of requests for donations. The average American believer is barraged with appeals for funds. Most of the appeals come from legitimate, Christ-honoring organizations and individuals who genuinely need financial support. But many believers become worn out by so many asking for so much when they have so little.

By learning and applying biblical principles of giving, the Christian can make a significant contribution to the Lord's work, and enjoy doing it. By basing his giving on scriptural guidelines rather than a purely emotional response to appeals, the believer can experience pleasure rather than pressure.

Before we discuss biblical principles and priorities for giving, I want to evaluate two common approaches to giving: the tithe and the faith promise.

### The Tithe

More than one Stewardship Sunday sermon has been preached on the text of Malachi 3:8-10:

> "Will a man rob God? Yet you rob me.
> But you ask, 'How do we rob you?'
> In tithes and offerings. You are under a curse—the whole nation of you—because you are robbing me.

Bring the whole tithe into the storehouse, that there may be food in my house. Test me in this," says the LORD Almighty, "and see if I will not throw open the floodgates of heaven and pour out so much blessing that you will not have room enough for it."

Tithing, a system of financial support employed in Israel during the Old Testament age, is practiced by many Christians today. It has the advantages of simplicity, consistency, and discipline. The believer contributes 10 percent of his income to the church, and the church makes all the decisions on distribution. Tithing follows a biblical pattern and generates considerable revenue in those churches where a high percentage of members practice it. Most people who tithe feel they are doing so in obedience to God's command. And many believe their financial prosperity is conditioned upon faithfulness in tithing.

There is nothing wrong with giving a tenth of one's income to the Lord. However, a fuller understanding of the place of tithing in God's overall program will put such a practice in its proper perspective.

The text from Malachi contains several points that deserve comment. Note the following: (1) Failure to bring the designated tithes constituted theft from God; (2) the command was to bring the whole tithe; (3) it was to be brought to the temple; (4) the temple was to serve as a storehouse, not only for funds, but for food; and (5) as disobedience brought a curse, so obedience would bring material blessing.

Malachi should not have had to bring such a message to Israel. Moses had already done so. It was all contained in Israel's Law. The temple-based ministry was to be supported by the tithes of the people.

Because they were required, the tithes of Israel were more like taxes than gifts. That is why failure to submit the "whole tithe" could be described as "robbing God." Furthermore, if one of God's people wanted to express his worship through a voluntary offering, it had to be over and above the tithe he owed (Deut. 12:6,11; 1 Chron. 29:6-9, 14). An offering cannot be "freewill" if it is commanded.

## Planned Obsolescence

The tithe, which was foundational to the economic system of the theocratic nation of Israel, is *not* part of the economic system of the church. In the church, there are no taxes, dues, membership fees, or any other prescribed assessments. The ministry of the church is supported as each member gives "what he has decided in his heart to give, not reluctantly or under compulsion" (2 Cor. 9:7). And so, Christians are not under obligation to practice tithing.

This is so for several reasons: (1) The local church does not have the same function as the temple did—the church is not a storehouse; (2) the material blessing that was promised as a reward for faithfulness in the Old Testament is not promised to the saints of this age; (3) according to the apostles, the Mosaic Law was expressly set aside for Christians; and (4) the command to tithe is not carried over into New Testament revelation.

In summary, while the practice of tithing has some advantages, that approach to giving is not prescribed for Christians. The Old Testament pattern is no longer operational. Believers today couldn't obey Malachi 3:8-10 if they wanted to. In the New Testament, the principle of tithing was replaced by the principle of grace giving.

## The Tithe: An Unequal Yoke

An understanding of these truths is important, for some Christians need to be set free from the *burden* of tithing, while others need to be released from the *limitations* of giving a mere tenth. David Hocking illustrates:

> Here are two men, one who makes $1,000 a year, and one who makes $100,000 a year. The first man gives 10% and he has $900 left to live on; the second man gives 10% and he has $90,000 to live on. That's a far cry from $900! Perhaps the econo-

my only demands $900 to live on; or perhaps $9000 would be more like it. The first man would suffer greatly, while the second would not have a care financially.

Consistent application of the New Testament principle of proportional giving would eliminate such inequities and actually increase the total amount given by Christians for the Lord's work.

## The Faith Promise

A second contemporary system of giving is called the "faith promise." While explanations of the approach differ in detail, the distinctive features of the plan are as follows: (1) God is the Supplier of the money, the believer is blessed by the privilege of being his channel; (2) the money to be given is to be "over and above" all existing giving commitments; (3) the amount to be given is determined by God and revealed subjectively to the believer in response to faith and prayer; (4) the money is supplied as the Christian continues to trust God for it; (5) the money will come from unexpected sources; and (6) the destination of the gift is already determined—by the organization that explains the approach.

Faith promise giving assumes that God has already determined a certain amount of money that he wants the believer to give. Through prayer and inward impressions of the Holy Spirit, God is expected to reveal that specific amount to the believer.

### Nothing Succeeds Like Success

As a system of giving, the faith promise method is quite popular. Churches have found that a properly run faith promise program increases giving to missions. Mission organizations are able to raise remarkable totals from a single banquet where their work is described and the faith promise method is explained. And they are able to do so without siphoning off funds from other essential ministries.

As a system, the faith promise approach to giving is not a biblical plan. But it works, in large measure because it incorporates two principles that are thoroughly biblical. First, the method greatly encourages prayer. Picture the college student who "in faith" concludes that God wants him to give $300 to the missionary project beyond all his regular giving. This student is motivated to pray! Many who commit themselves to a faith promise begin to pray with earnest intensity for the first time. God responds to such prayer whether it is part of a faith promise program or not. Second, the method encourages great generosity. This too is biblical. Generosity pleases the heart of God whether it is part of a faith promise program or not.

## Choose a Number

Faith promise giving has some flaws that are in need of correction. Foremost of these is that the method lacks a scriptural basis. The reason the method is so productive of spiritual results is not because the system as a whole is valid, but because people are challenged to pray and give generously. God honors obedience to those biblical principles, just as he blesses all obedience to his Word.

But parts of the method are doctrinally fallacious. The first problem is the process of determining the amount to be pledged. God does not reveal his individual will for our decisions through inner impressions (for a complete discussion about how to find God's will, see *Decision Making and the Will of God* by Garry Friesen with J. Robin Maxson). It is not surprising that for some people, a whole jumble of figures come to mind, while others draw a blank and are not "impressed" by any amount at all.

Instead of deciding on the basis of some mystical inner impression, the believer is to make such decisions on the basis of specific guidelines in accordance with established priorities. These are set forth in Scripture and will be discussed more fully later.

### Promises, Promises

A second problem relates to the nature of faith. Faith promise giving encourages Christians to trust God for something he has not said he will do—namely, come up with a specific amount of money for a specific project within a certain period of time. No verse in the Bible indicates that God has promised this. To hold God to a promise he hasn't put on the record isn't faith—it is presumption. Genuine faith must be anchored to verifiable promises. That is what characterized Abraham, who was "fully persuaded that God had power to do what he had promised" (Rom. 4:21). If God doesn't promise, we can't promise. And an inward impression is not a promise.

Because of these biblical deficiencies, participants in a faith promise program come to false conclusions. Those who are able to meet their pledges give glory to God and conclude that the system is valid. But the success of the program does not prove its validity. Only Scripture can do that. Those who don't meet their quota, though they are just as prayerful and generous, end up wondering if their faith is weak. Not only is that an inappropriate response, but it robs the giver of joy in giving what God did provide and replaces that joy with false guilt.

There are two other possible explanations for failure to meet one's faith promise: either God didn't come through, or there is something wrong with the system. We have concluded that the faith promise format needs modification to bring it into alignment with Scripture.

### Seven Hundred Dollars Short on Faith

When I was in college, I participated in a faith promise project. When the appeal was made, the only figure that came to my mind was $1000. I didn't have that kind of money. If I sold everything I had (and I did try to sell a few things), I could not raise $1000. So I prayed and worked.

What I was able to contribute was $300. That was fantastic! I had never given like that in my life. But I was more frustrated than joyful because I was $700 short on faith. I needed to learn that God hadn't promised to give me $1000. That figure was the product of my own mind. What the Lord did expect me to do was to pray fervently, gratefully accept what he chose to provide, and give generously.

When I went to seminary, I attempted to apply some of the lessons I had been learning about faith, prayer, and giving. I desired to minister in a particular church where the people could not pay me. To do that, I would need $2000 per semester from other sources. I did not have time to work at another (paying) job and do this ministry, so I prayed and asked God to provide the $2000.

No verse in the Bible said God had to give me that $2000. No passage exempted me from gainful employment. Most of my seminary brothers had to work at one or more outside jobs, and there would be nothing wrong with me working for pay somewhere. I was willing to do that and would thank the Lord if he chose to provide for my needs in such a manner.

But the Lord chose to answer my prayer positively. He provided that $2000 per semester through the gifts of other believers, and I was able to minister in that church without being a burden to those people. God provided the needed money, not because I had a foolproof system, not because I had more faith than anyone else, not because he was obligated to come up with the amount that came to my mind, but because he is gracious and because he answers prayer.

The two situations I have described are dissimilar in several respects. But they share a common bottom line: Money had to be provided if a ministry was to function. And what I learned from the first incident helped me to better approach the second. I avoided the mistake of locking God into a box of my own construction. I asked him to provide an income in some manner that would free me to minister without pay. Then I left the outcome to him. The figure I asked for was not extracted from thin air, but based on specific, anticipated needs. Because God is wiser than we are, the way he chooses to provide will be wiser. And by letting him act with no strings attached, he gets the glory regardless of the outcome.

## Biblical Principles of Giving

### Purposeful, Proportionate Giving

We've said enough about what biblical principles of giving aren't. Now we need to see what they are. The most extended treatment of giving in the New Testament is found in 2 Corinthians 8 and 9. You would do well to carefully read those chapters before continuing on with this material.

The decisions each believer must make about giving are numerous. Among them are determining how much of one's income to give, and how to distribute what is given. Since we have been discussing various ways of determining the amount to be given, we will look first at those passages that address that issue.

In 2 Corinthians 8 and 9, the phrases that relate to the matter of choosing an amount to give are very instructive:

- "as much as they were able" (8:3)
- "entirely on their own" (8:3)
- "according to your means" (8:11)
- "according to what one has, not according to what he does not have" (8:12).

All of these expressions are consistent with the summary exhortation of 2 Corinthians 9:7: "Each man should give what he has decided in his heart to give, not reluctantly or under compulsion, for God loves a cheerful giver." This verse rules out the compulsion of a required tithe. It also speaks against the extracting of contributions by means of pressure, guilt trips, or emotional manipulation. The matter is placed squarely on the shoulders of the individual believer who is to give "what he has decided in his heart to give." There is no hint of any inward impression; no instruction to seek for clues to God's will. This verse *is* God's will for our giving.

The same point is made in different words in 1 Corinthians 16:2: "On the first day of every week, each one of you should set aside a sum of money *in keeping with his income*, saving it up, so that when I come no collections will have to be made." Under grace, the tithe has been replaced by the principle of proportionate giving.

It is not difficult to compute 10 percent of one's income; but how much is "in keeping with his income"? It is neither a specific amount nor a particular percentage. The rich should be "rich in good deeds" (1 Tim. 6:17-18). Those who have nothing are not expected to give anything (2 Cor. 8:12). Those who have less than enough are to receive from others who have more than enough (8:13-14). Those who have little give the little that they can (8:2-3). Increasing prosperity should result not only in an increase in the amount given, but in the percentage given. Many Americans should think about giving 15, 20, 40, or 60 percent of their income. Their abundance should make them abundant givers.

## The Rich Young Giver

When I was pastoring in a church, a young man in the congregation came to talk to me about giving. He said, "I used to think the reason I did not give much was because I did not have much. But now that I have quite a bit of money, I still find I am not giving much. How should I give?"

I explained to him the principles of grace giving. Then I suggested he select a percentage of his income consistent with the degree to which the Lord had blessed him financially. In one week, I promised to follow up our conversation by asking him if he had chosen a percentage to give to the Lord.

A week later I checked with him. "Yes," he replied, "I think that 40 percent is about right." I gulped. From next to nothing to 40 percent is a big jump. Nevertheless, I encouraged him to follow his plan for one month and then evaluate. If he felt some adjustment was called for after that trial period, he could change the amount if he wished.

At the end of the month, we discussed his giving. He was full of joy and said it had been a great period in his Christian life. He had invested significantly in the Lord's work and had derived great satisfaction from his giving. Moreover, his new commitment to giving was requiring him to more carefully budget the rest of his money. He was amazed at how much he had formerly wasted on things he did not need.

When I suggested that he reconsider the percentage of his income he would give the following month, he readily agreed. "I have concluded that 40 percent is too little in view of the way God has been prospering me. This month, I think 60 percent would be more appropriate."

Later, I overheard one of the young people talking about this same brother. "You know, he doesn't spend away his money like he used to. I wonder what's gotten into him." I knew the answer. He was learning to give rather than waste. Abundant giving and careful spending were his new response to God's prospering of his life.

## Principles of Grace Giving

The principle of proportionate giving is a needed corrective to other, less biblical approaches. But that principle will be inadequately understood and subject to abuse if it is not seen within the context of other New Testament guidelines for giving. We cannot fully develop all of these principles here, but the following outline, developed primarily from 2 Corinthians 8 and 9, provides a helpful overview for further study.

1. God himself is the Model, Motivator, and Equipper of all Christian giving (2 Cor. 8:9; 9:8-10,15).

2. Giving one's money to the Lord is an extension of the prior gift of one's self (2 Cor. 8:5; Rom. 12:1-2). The donation of a portion of one's wealth is made in the recognition that everything the believer has belongs to God (1 Cor. 4:7; 6:19-20; Luke 19:11-27; 1 Chron. 29:14).

3. The ability and motivation to give to the Lord is a function of grace (2 Cor. 8:1-3,6-7; 9:8-10). Grace is that

work of God in the believer that gives both the desire and the power to fulfill God's will.

4. In God's eyes, the *attitude* of the giver is more important than the *amount* given (2 Cor. 9:7). Accordingly, grace giving is to be characterized by joy (2 Cor. 8:2), cheerfulness (9:7), liberality (8:2), sacrifice (8:2-3), eagerness (8:4,7-8; 9:2), willingness (8:12), perseverance (8:10-12), and integrity (8:20-21).

5. Giving is a spiritual exercise in which *all* believers may participate, even poor ones (2 Cor. 8:2; Luke 21:1-4).

6. The value of a gift is not determined by its amount but by its cost (2 Cor. 8:2; Luke 21:1-4). The question should not be, "How much can I spare?" but rather, "How much can I sacrifice?" Not "How much can I give?" but, "How much can I give up?"

7. The believer is not expected to give more than he is able. Often, however, Christians find that they can give more than they thought they could afford (2 Cor. 8:3,12).

8. The extent of spiritual "treasure" or "fruit" is either limited or expanded by the extent of the gift (2 Cor. 9:6; Matt. 6:19-21).

9. The ability to give is granted by God, who gives even more to those who want to give more (2 Cor. 9:9-11; Luke 6:38).

10. The opportunity to give is to be viewed as a privilege, not a compulsory obligation (2 Cor. 8:4; 9:7).

11. The greatest threat to generous giving is not poverty but covetousness (Luke 12:13-34; Acts 5:1-10).

12. If a promise of financial support is made, every effort must be made to fulfill it (2 Cor. 8:10-12; 9:5).

13. The Christian's giving is to be regular, individual, systematic, proportionate (1 Cor. 16:1-2).

14. The results of grace giving will include:

- A harvest of righteousness (2 Cor. 9:10; Phil. 4:17)

- Further enrichment of the giver so that he can give more (2 Cor. 9:11)
- Thanksgiving to God (2 Cor. 9:11-12)
- The meeting of needs (2 Cor. 9:12)
- The praising of God (2 Cor. 9:13)
- Verification of the message of the gospel (2 Cor. 9:13; John 13:35)
- The offering of reciprocal prayers (2 Cor. 9:14)
- A strengthening of the bonds of fellowship between believers (2 Cor. 9:14)

### Biblical Priorities in Giving

Once one has decided how much of his income he wishes to give to the Lord, it remains for him to determine the distribution of those funds. Guidance for this decision is provided in the New Testament where priorities are set forth for the use of our money.

### Charity Begins at Home

Heading the list of priorities is one's *family*. Paul wrote, "If anyone does not provide for his relatives, and especially for his immediate family, he has denied the faith and is worse than an unbeliever" (1 Tim. 5:8). Those are strong words—even for Paul! One's immediate family is given the highest priority for financial provision, as is indicated by the word "especially."

The second sphere of responsibility encompasses one's wider family, or *relatives*. In 1 Timothy 5, much of the discussion centers on the proper care of widows. Paul stresses that the primary responsibility for such care falls on the immediate family rather than the church: "But if a widow has children or grandchildren, these should learn first of all to put their religion into practice by caring for their own family and so repaying their parents and grandparents, for this is pleasing to God" (1 Tim. 5:4; see 5:16).

### Don't Muzzle the Ox—or the Preacher

The believer also has a financial responsibility to provide for those who are ministering the Word to him. "Anyone who receives instruction in the word must share all good things with his instructor" (Gal. 6:6). If those who receive such spiritual ministry fail to provide for the sustenance of the teacher, he will have to curtail his teaching and find other means to support himself and his family. This would lead to the spiritual impoverishment of the church. To be sure, no man is to become a pastor for the purpose of gaining wealth (1 Pet. 5:2). But the one who preaches the gospel is entitled to make his living thereby (1 Cor. 9:11,14; 1 Tim. 5:17-18).

There are some situations, however, in which it is simply not possible for a man to receive a living wage from those he is ministering to. A new and struggling work often cannot fully support a pastor. An evangelist or missionary reaching into an unevangelized area cannot expect local unbelievers to take up an offering. Thus, we have the opportunity and necessity of providing financial support for those who are ministering to other people in other places.

### Robbing Macedonia to Feed Corinth

Such monetary assistance was probably included as part of the church's role in sending out the first two missionaries, Barnabas and Saul (Acts 13:2-3). The believers in the infant church at Philippi began giving to help Paul in his church planting ministry shortly after they were saved (Phil. 4:15-16). The immaturity of the Christians in Corinth forced Paul to rely on gifts from other churches to sustain his ministry there. Paul later wrote to these Corinthians,

> I robbed other churches by receiving support from them so as to serve you. And when I was with you and needed something, I was not a burden to anyone, for the brothers who came from Macedonia supplied what I needed. I have kept myself from

being a burden to you in any way, and will continue to do so (2 Cor. 11:8-9).

By Paul's reckoning, the responsibility for his support belonged to the saints he was ministering to—the Corinthians. Because they neglected to provide for him, he "robbed" other churches for his support. On the other hand, he commended the believers from Macedonia for supplying his needs, even though he was not ministering directly to them.

From the very outset of the church's missionary activity, local churches have viewed financial support of missionaries as a means of direct involvement in the fulfillment of the Great Commission. Thus, a church and its members are expected to first support the ministry to themselves, and then to participate financially in the gospel-spreading work of other messengers in other places (see Acts 1:8).

### Rescue the Perishing

Giving to meet physical needs is another responsibility that received emphasis in the ministry of Christ and his apostles (Gal. 6:10; 1 John 3:17). In fact, all of Paul's exhortation in 2 Corinthians 8-9, from which the church derives many of its principles of giving, was directed toward the collection of relief funds for the impoverished saints in Judea.

The priorities that have been established for the relief of the poor are: believers first, unbelievers second. The needy in one's spiritual family take precedence over those in the world. We may not neglect the needs of unbelievers by caring exclusively for our own. It is not a case of either/or, but of both/and. Paul said, "Therefore, as we have opportunity, let us do good to all people, especially to those who belong to the family of believers" (Gal. 6:10).

To sum up: As the Christian responds to the grace of God by being a good steward of his money, he determines the distribution of his funds according to biblical priorities. In general, the order of his giving moves outward, with those who are closest to him having the priority of provision: the immediate family, the extended family, the work of the local church, the work of gospel proclamation, and, finally, the relief of needy believers, then unbelievers. Such an order in giving is part of a sound strategy for outreach. For the long-term support of missionary activity requires the prior establishment of a solid base of operations at home.

## Passing Out God's Money Is Fun

In recent years, I have adopted the following approach to my practice of giving. I have chosen a percentage of my income that I contribute to the Lord's work. A portion of what I give goes to my local church to sustain the ministry of those who are sharing the Word with me. I have also decided that half of what I give will go to ministries where the gospel is being proclaimed through evangelism, church planting, and other missionary enterprises. Some of this giving can be channeled through the local church, and some can go directly to the persons or agencies I have a personal interest in.

When it comes to giving money to meet physical needs, I used to get all tensed up. The reason, quite simply, is that there are so many needs—many more than I could ever hope to meet. I felt guilty every time I heard a moving story of someone's plight, or saw a picture of starving people. I found I was being motivated almost entirely by the pull of my emotions, rather than responding to the instructions of Scripture.

So I determined that about 10 percent of the money I give to the Lord will go for the meeting of needs. I have established what I call the "Need Fund." Every payday, the appropriate amount of money is put aside in that fund. That money is devoted for the Lord's use to meet needs. Whenever I learn of a need, if there is money in my "Need Fund," I have the joy of passing it out. And if there is nothing in that fund when I learn of a need, I don't have to feel guilty about not giving.

Of course, I'm not restricted to giving only what's in that fund. If the situation warrants it, I can divert moneys that were earmarked for other purposes to meet an urgent need. Some circumstances call for sacrificial giving. Sometimes, when I hear of a special need and the reserves are depleted, I ask the Lord to provide some additional money that I can give. If he chooses to do so, I have the joy of passing it along. And if he doesn't, I can trust him to supply that need through other channels.

God has entrusted to his children the privilege and responsibility of wisely utilizing this world's goods to attain spiritual fruit. The freedom that Christians have to make decisions about giving can be exploited by some for their own selfish needs. But not for long. For God is not mocked—a man will reap what he sows (Gal. 6:6-10). And those who freely give as they have freely received will experience great joy and blessing as recipients of God's abundant grace.

Thanks be to God for his indescribable gift!
(2 Cor. 9:15).

### CrossCheck

1. Do you agree with the author's conclusion that the tithe and the faith promise are not in keeping with New Testament principles of giving? Why or why not?

2. What is the principle of proportionate giving? Do you think this principle is more in keeping with New Testament teaching?

3. What did Jesus mean when he said, "It is more blessed to give than to receive"? Describe a time when you experienced what Jesus was talking about.

4. What changes, if any, in your giving practices are you considering after reading this chapter?


Garry Friesen is dean of faculty at Multnomah Bible College in Portland, Oregon. He is a graduate of Dallas Theological Seminary and the author of *Decision Making and the Will of God: A Biblical Alternative to the Traditional View*.

# CHAPTER 6

# Fellowship

## *Karl I. Payne*

*I just don't feel like I know anyone or that anybody cares about me. I come and I go, and nobody notices.*

*At my old church I could share anything and know that people would listen, care, and pray for me. Here I feel like I might as well be talking to myself. It is so cold.*

When was the last time you heard someone make comments similar to these? Perhaps you have caught yourself making these kinds of statements, or at least thinking them.

I will never forget the bewilderment my wife and I felt trying to find a new church as excited newlyweds. We had recently moved six hundred miles away from our families and home church to begin my seminary training. We assumed that finding a church would be easy and that congregations would be eager to have seminary students join their ranks. We quickly found out that both assumptions were wrong. We left the warmth, familiarity, and security of our home and friends and felt as though we walked into an ice storm.

The Christian faith is supposed to be a family affair. Christians were never meant to live in isolation from the world or from each other. Paul made this abundantly clear in Romans 12 and 1 Corinthians 12 where he compares the Christian body to a human body. Eyes, ears, feet, hands—we need them all. The various parts of the body must work as complements to one another. Put simply, we need each other.

Just what does this have to do with the Christian's need for fellowship? A great deal. Today individual rights and freedoms are assumed to always be virtues. Living for one's self and for the moment are a primary goal for most people. Independence to do what I want, when I want, regardless of the ramifications, is viewed as normal living. Self-sacrifice for the needs of others is considered naive and a waste of time. Statements such as "It's my right," or "What will it cost me?" have replaced "Is it right?" or "How will this decision affect others?" Given this independent and shortsighted focus, biblical fellowship often is the victim of schedules that are short on time and resistant to personal inconvenience.

## The Components of Fellowship

Fellowship is easier to define than it is to implement. It is one thing to define fellowship, but quite another matter to see it fleshed out. What are the essential elements of fellowship that we need to understand and implement if we are to experience the reality of fellowship rather than simply long for it? Genuine fellowship involves caring, sharing, giving, encouraging, exhorting, and self-sacrifice. Let's briefly examine these necessary components.

### Fellowship involves caring

I recently asked a friend why he left a church I had recommended he attend. His answer broke my heart. After attending regularly with his wife for some time and still feeling like a visitor, he decided to introduce himself to three new people every Sunday. He reasoned that if members would not take the initiative to make new people feel welcome, he would. After months of this effort, the only person who ever greeted him or made any attempt to reciprocate was a businessman asking for a donation for the local Christian radio station he worked for. The church he is now attending is weak theologically by comparison to the one he left, but I will never forget his response when I mentioned this to him. He said, "Karl, the big church is built around the pastor, and he is a good man. But the established people do not care about new people. At our new church, even though it is smaller and the preacher is not as strong, they have let us know that they care about us and need us."

A congregation of Christians can be orthodox in their theology, but sterile and removed from the needs and feelings of members and visitors. Fellowship is not primarily a head issue; it is first and foremost a matter of the heart. Do I care about the needs of others? The caring that is necessary for fellowship to occur is a choice. The decision to reach out to others or to allow another person to reach into my life is deliberate. Self-sacrifice and self-centeredness are both choices. I can choose to focus on others, as described in Philippians 2:4, or I can choose to focus on myself.

How do you express care for others at home, work, or in your church? Do your words, intonation, and body language express care and invite others to build friendships, or do you plant "Private—Keep out" signposts? Individuals or churches who desire to see fellowship become a reality must say to others, "We care," "You are valuable," "We want to get to know you," and "We need each other." Fellowship cannot and will not develop apart from people expressing care and love for others.

When someone is hurting, do you have to be asked to get involved? If new people join your group or move into your neighborhood, do you extend a friendly hand to make sure they feel welcomed? An attitude of care usually translates into looking for God-given opportunities to help others. Caring people do not have to be asked to get involved; they assume reaching out is the right thing to do. If we treat others the way we hope they treat us, we will extend ourselves to them without being asked.

Caring, loving, and reaching out to others is risky because these actions can be misunderstood or rejected. But those who desire to see fellowship become a reality must be willing to take the risk. The failure to take this risk is contributing to declining church attendance from coast to coast.

A few years ago, I was on the pastoral staff of a large church in the Northwest. I will never forget the way one group in that body demonstrated its love and care for a person who would normally have been ignored at best, or made the butt of jokes and taken advantage of at worst.

Lyle was probably in his midtwenties, but he had the mental capabilities of a child of five or six. I fully expected the young adults his age to shun him. He was offensive at times in his speech and could not keep up with the group. But I watched the members of that group consistently provide love, friendship, and a family atmosphere that shouted out, "Lyle, you belong. We love you and will protect you." When ball teams were picked, Lyle was always chosen, and never last. New people to the group who thought they could impress others by taking verbal cheap shots at Lyle usually made that mistake only once. The unspoken but understood attitude of the group declared: "We are family. You can't attack our members without attacking our group as well."

Lyle did far more for the atmosphere of that group than he will ever understand. When new people entering the group saw the way Lyle was treated and the obvious love members had for one another, their facades crumbled quickly. The group was real because the individuals in it were caring Christians who chose to create an atmosphere where people received more attention than the obstacles they brought in with them. Members of that group knew they would be accepted, warts and all. "Lyles" have a way of reminding us how fragile we are and just how much we need each other.

Genuine fellowship begins with an attitude of caring, an attitude that cannot be faked for very long. It involves a willingness to reach out to others. People who care do not have to be told to get involved with others; they look for opportunities to do so. They are not self-serving.

### Fellowship involves sharing.

For genuine fellowship to occur, we must feel the freedom to share our heart without fear of rejection or reprisal. Confidential matters are seldom shared among casual acquaintances. If a person is burned for sharing his heart with others, he will not usually make himself vulnerable again, at least to the ones who hurt him. Self-serving and self-centered protectionism is normal to fallen human nature, but it destroys the freedom and openness necessary for the honest sharing needed in fellowship.

Christian fellowship should provide a safe harbor, a place we can go to get out of the waves that toss us to and fro as we try to navigate the tricky and potentially destructive hazards of daily living. Safe harbors provide a calm in the storm that enables us to regroup, recoup, and refuel before pressing on. But just as the atmosphere created by caring attitudes does not happen by accident, neither will harbors of safety. Safe harbors are created through daily choices made by people who desire to treat others the way they themselves wish to be treated.

Can someone share something confidential with you and know the matter will stay between the two of you and God? Do you actively seek to make the group you are a part of a safe harbor? Can wounded spiritual warriors talk about their discouragements and set-backs as well as their victories and still be treated with respect? When someone asks you for prayer, do you pray for them—or talk to others about your prayer ministry for them? Genuine fellowship will develop between individuals when they feel confident that the things they share will produce help and not hurt.

Julie and Jennifer both liked the same young man. All three were active members of a Bible study I was leading. During a prayer and praise session before the study, Julie calmly said to the group, "I think we should pray that Jennifer is not pregnant." I asked Julie if there was a good reason she was raising this prayer request for her friend. (The boy they both liked was present that night, but Jennifer was not.) She said she just wanted us to pray for her friend. I told Julie we would pray that Jennifer was not pregnant if we could also pray that she was not pregnant. She responded, "But what would people think of me if we do that?" I said, "Probably the same thing you're wanting us to think about Jennifer."

Julie decided that the whole idea was not such a good

one and wished she had never brought the subject up. I agreed, but I also took the time to explain that if not confronted in love, this type of manipulating prayer was guaranteed to destroy a friendship and make a mockery of loving intercession. She knew she had blown it, and the group did, too. But the genuine fellowship experienced in the group allowed instruction to turn potentially destructive slander into a terrific object lesson and a time of loving correction.

The things shared by that group were consistently genuine and the fellowship was real. For many it was the only caring family they had ever experienced and the only place they knew they could reveal their heart without being ridiculed. The Christian faith is a family affair and members who do not love and protect one another are living in disobedience to God.

Fellowship will not occur outside the context of a safe harbor where people know that the things they share will bring healing and not harm. Gossips die friendless. People who cannot keep a confidence are gossips whose unchecked actions will destroy any hope for genuine fellowship.

## Fellowship involves giving

It is difficult to convince people they are cared for if their world is crumbling around them and no one is willing to help. Genuine fellowship involves a willingness to help meet the needs of others. Fellowship that consistently fails to meet emotional and material concerns as well as spiritual and eternal ones is not complete.

You may be wondering, "How can I be involved in giving that will contribute toward fellowship?" Giving can and will take many forms. It may be helping a family in a financial bind, or mowing their lawn and picking up their mail while they are on vacation. The giving of genuine fellowship is a sacrificial choice that willingly helps meet the needs of others. Consistently praying for a friend is the most important thing I can ever do for him or her, but sometimes God gives me the resources to be the answer to my friend's prayers.

The book of Acts reveals that besides breaking bread, listening to the apostles teaching, and praying together, one of the practices of the early church was for Christians who had material means to provide for those who did not. The issue was not whether the people involved were best friends or business partners, but whether they were fellow members of the body of Christ in need.

I am not talking here about giving to people we have never met or who have a reputation for abusing generosity. I am talking about helping fellow family members and friends in the body of Christ who are in need.

The members of our college group care deeply for one another, and the fellowship they experience is exciting. Many affectionately refer to their group as "the family." One Sunday morning I told the class that our evangelism ministry team needed funds for more gospel tracts and Bibles. A hat was passed to help meet the need, and the group gave three hundred dollars on the spot to purchase more materials. One person from the class approached me a short time later and made arrangements to purchase ten thousand gospel tracts. For Thanksgiving one of the local collegians opened his house for a get together for anyone who wanted to come, but particularly targeted college students who were away from home and had nowhere to go for the holiday.

Heart-felt fellowship is by no means limited to collegians. I know of another Sunday school class that is a sterling example of giving as a by-product of fellowship. Time and again the group has voluntarily taken offerings over and above their normal giving to help fellow members who have lost their job, face unexpected medical bills, or are needing financial help for a ministry project. "Amens" ring out when praises are expressed for answered prayer, and tears flow freely as honest hurts are shared. The women have prepared meals and the men have helped with handyman needs so often it no longer seems unusual.

Giving to help meet needs is one practical aspect of fellowship. Although giving will not earn or merit God's eternal favor, sacrificial giving is a pragmatic way of demonstrating that God is working in a person's life. Generally, when God has control of our wallet, he also has control of our heart and mind. Fellowship involves giving.

## Fellowship involves encouraging.

When you think of a biblical character who was an encourager, who do you think of? The first person I think of is Barnabas. The name Barnabas means "Son of Encouragement," according to Acts 4:36. When the early Christians were afraid to accept Paul after his conversion because his reputation as a persecutor preceded him, who was the one leader willing to stand up for him and encourage him in the faith? Barnabas (Acts 9). When the poverty of the saints in Jerusalem became apparent, who chose to sell land he owned and give the entire proceeds to help meet the needs of the poor? Barnabas (Acts 4). When Paul refused to take Mark on his second missionary journey because of his failure during the first trip, who left Paul to nurse Mark back to spiritual productivity? Barnabas (Acts 15).

Encouragers are individuals who consistently demonstrate the type of attitude and lifestyle commanded in Philippians 2:3-4.

> Do nothing out of selfish ambition or vain conceit, but in humility consider others better than yourselves. Each of you should look not only to your own interests, but also to the interests of others.

Encouragers see potential and possibilities in others rather than failure. They believe and look for the best rather than assume the worst. Encouragers are more interested in seeing others receive strokes than in being stroked. Encouragers respond to need and are not nearly as concerned about being inconvenienced as they are about helping others. Encouragers are usually people-oriented rather than product-oriented; they consider self-sacrifice a normal part of Christian living. Encouragers are solid as rocks under pressure and see adversity as a challenge to rise above rather than a reason to quit.

Encouragement is a vital ingredient for genuine fellowship. We all need encouragement at times. Just as a person with a judgmental attitude can cripple himself and infect those around him, so too an encourager can lift the attitude and spirit of an individual or an entire group. This world will never know how many people who achieved greatness were urged by an encourager to keep trying after initial failures, or how many gifted people who could have excelled gave up because no one believed in them and encouraged them to try again. A word, a look, a touch, a smile, a brief compliment, all can be agents of encouragement. Encouragement comes in a variety of manners, but in its effective way it says, "By God's grace you can."

One day just hours before our summer mission team was to pull out of the church parking lot, one of the leaders approached me and said, "Karl, I can't go. You just don't understand." He told me later that he had already decided to pack it up and go home. I told him, "I may not understand everything you are feeling, but I know good men and how to train them for ministry. You are a good man and equipped for the job or I wouldn't let you go." He reluctantly climbed into the back of one of our vans. He not only did a tremendous job that summer, he went out with the team three or four more years. He eventually married one of the staff members who just happened to be on that first mission trip. He is an honor student in Bible school, planning on attending seminary after graduation, and wanting to go into full-time vocational Christian ministry. You never know what an appropriate word of encouragement at the right time will help accomplish, by God's grace.

Earlier we talked about the importance of creating a safe harbor where individuals can share their innermost feelings and thoughts without the fear of rejection. Encouragement is directly related to this safe harbor concept. The words of an encourager are not always soft or easy, but they can be counted on to be in the best interests of the one needing encouragement.

Have you ever been encouraged by someone when you felt like you were on the bottom looking up? Has a concerned person assured you that you are valuable and cared for when you felt worthless and all alone? Aren't you glad someone was willing to make the effort to encourage you? Can you think of a time when you needed to be encouraged and no one was willing or available to help? Would you have appreciated a caring, confrontive friend at that time? Who are you encouraging right now? Who do you know who needs someone to tell them, "You can make it and I'm going to stand with you"? Are you the kind of friend who can be counted on to help pick a struggling Christian soldier up?

Too often, even as Christians, we feel we are being pounded by the waves of life, rather than riding on top of them. It's okay to need and accept help. We are family. Fellowship involves encouragement from other believers who remind us that we are not alone and that we will make it.

### Fellowship involves exhortation.

Ken was a student loaded with potential, but he was undisciplined and lazy. One afternoon as he sprawled on a chair in my office, I said to him, "Ken, you are one of the most gifted individuals I have met, but you are lazy and undisciplined. If you do not decide to grow up, you are going to be buried with a tombstone that says, *He had such potential.*" His response was unforgettable. He said, "I have known that's true all my life, but you are the only one who has ever confronted me on it." Our relationship had developed to a point where honest conversations were appreciated by both of us. His response to confrontation was positive. He became more than just a "potential" asset for the work of Christ.

Genuine fellowship involves more than providing spiritual stitches for a person who has been hurt. It also involves godly counsel on how to avoid problems in the first place. Exhortation can be a pleasant assignment or an opportunity to risk a relationship, depending on the attitude of the exhorter and the response of the one being exhorted. But genuine fellowship cares enough to confront when exhortation is necessary.

Exhortation is often thought of as a spiritual gift that allows a person to be lovingly confrontive, pragmatic, encouraging, clear, and straight forward. But we need not feel we must have a particular spiritual gift to express loving, confrontive advice for a friend. Parents often function in the role of exhorter to their children, hoping to help them avoid potential problems. "Jonathan, you must hold mommy's or daddy's hand when you cross the street. We do not want a car to hit you." "Honey, if you tease the dog, he is going to bite you. Leave him alone." "Jill, he is using you. If you don't get out of this relationship soon, your emotional motor will be revving so fast you won't be able to get out without tremendous hurt."

One of my boyhood friends informed me one afternoon that, after eleven years of marriage and two young children, God had told him to divorce his wife. I told him that God would not tell him to do this. His response and rationale was a classic. He said, "I am just no good for Sherry. I figure the only way she is ever going to be happy is if I get out of her life and give her a chance to start over." He was serious. I suggested to him that rather than break up his family and renege on his vows, it would be more honest if he would decide to be the godly father and husband he knew he was supposed to be. I told him that God would not command him to take this destructive action, but that a spiritual accuser might. He asked me, "What does the Bible say about divorce?" We started working through the Bible, looking at verses on divorce. An hour later he looked at me and said, "You're right. God would never have told me to do this." My friend decided to begin once again working on his marriage and his Christian life rather than cop out and blame God for his compromise.

I was lovingly exhorting my friend. It was not easy, but it

was necessary. Exhortation is a part of genuine fellowship, but it assumes that a relationship has been developed to a degree that difficult issues as well as pleasant ones can be addressed.

Have you developed friendships where you know you can speak honestly with each other? Can you discuss uncomfortable as well as enjoyable issues? It is difficult to accept exhortation from a person you don't know or whose motives you are unsure of. Relationships develop into fellowship through honest effort and time spent together. What are you doing to make sure fellowship is occurring in your friendships, small group, or church?

## Fellowship involves self-sacrifice.

Caring enough about people to reprioritize your busy schedule to help meet their need usually means self-sacrifice. To say that this is not always convenient is an understatement. But how important is fellowship to your own spiritual health and the well-being of others God has given you relationships with? And was the one who left us an example for godly living willing to be inconvenienced for the benefit of others?

Fellowship involves self-sacrifice, but what an example we have to follow (Heb. 12). Eternity is going to reveal the value God places on the self-sacrifice God's people have offered for the gospel's sake (Heb. 11).

To most Americans time is a valuable commodity. Most of us maintain schedules that are already overloaded; it's hard to find time to think or dream. Making time to think or dream for an entire family is even harder. But Christian fellowship asks us to develop caring, sharing, giving, encouraging, exhorting relationships that reach beyond our own families. In a Christian context, we become responsible not only for our immediate family, but also for every member of the small group or local church we have committed ourselves to. We are our brother's keeper.

Yet the give and take of fellowship can be extremely threatening. The transparency necessary for fellowship to be truly effective forces most of us to function outside our natural comfort zones. Genuine fellowship asks us to trust our most personal confidences to another. But we have a lifetime of learning, feelings, and experience which shout at us to hide, protect, and play it safe. Choosing to be aloof, alone, and isolated may be safe, but at what a cost!

Caring, sharing, giving, encouraging, exhorting, and self-sacrifice should be synonymous with Christian living. Christian living is a family affair and we really do need each other. However, with the fast-paced lifestyles we choose to live, and the superficial relationships we have learned to accept as normal, fellowship is often a reality longed for by many, but experienced by few.

### Do Most Christians Experience Genuine Christian Fellowship?

Most Christians are not experiencing Christian fellowship. Those who praise God because they have finally found a church where they feel accepted or a friend they can talk to and trust indict the rest of us for the norm we have learned to expect and accept.

> *At Chiggerville Bible Church they really care for one another. I was not there a week before the church sent people over to let me know how glad they were that I had come to one of their meetings. In less than a month I was plugged into a small group. It didn't take long before I knew that these people cared about me. Now we can share anything with each other and know we will still be loved and accepted. The fellowship is great. Come over and check things out. It really is different at Chiggerville!*

It is possible to find a place where fellowship is occurring, but fellowship among Christians should be the norm and not the exciting exception. Christian churches or small group fellowships are made up of individual Christians who have committed their lives to loving and serving their Savior, Jesus Christ. If we claim the same heavenly Father and are fellow members of the body of Christ, then we really are family. If we are family, we ought to be friends. If we are to share and feel each other's joys and sorrows as the Bible instructs us, we must care for and be committed to each other.

Our felt need for fellowship is real, but the sad truth is that for many of us, that need remains unmet. This simply must not be allowed to continue within the family of Christ. We must work together to make sure that lonely, isolated Christians become the exception, not the rule.

### Steps I Can Take to Ensure that I Experience Fellowship

Is it possible to guarantee that genuine Christian fellowship will occur in our relationships or at our church? No. Fellowship depends upon the motivation and action of at least two people. Although you cannot determine how others will contribute to meeting this need, you can decide how you will respond. What can I, as an individual, do to ensure that I am experiencing fellowship?

*1. Check your attitude.*

• Determine that time in your schedule to develop healthy relationships and friendships is vital, not optional. Growing relationships and friendships are the base on which fellowship will occur.

• Feelings of inadequacy, insecurity, pride, and fear can make moving out of our comfort zone predictably difficult. These natural feelings are common to man and, as such, Christians are not immune to them. Be courageous enough to reach out to others, even if you are afraid to try.

• Christians are equal in value to God. The payment was the same for each of us. We are all in the daily process of maturing as we are conformed to the image of Jesus Christ. We also share a common goal: to be equipped by faithful men for the work of service, for the building up of the body of Christ, to a mature and unified faith. We also desire to be doctrinally sound, able to speak the truth in love, and willing to make the contributions God has created us for so that the body of Christ will build itself in love.

• Remember that the felt need for fellowship is great, and in our mobile and impersonal society, it is difficult to have that need met even in the best of circumstances.

## 2. Commit yourself to helping create an atmosphere where fellowship will be considered normal rather than exceptional.

• Diligently work at making others feel welcome and accepted rather than planting "keep out" signs. Try viewing a situation through the eyes of a friend or a visitor. Care enough about others to try and make a difference. Healthy change usually begins with the thinking and action of one.

• Provide others the privilege of being able to fail without losing your respect. The greatest lessons we learn in the Christian life often come through failure. Even a casual read- ing of the Bible will show you that being able to learn through failure puts us in pretty good company. If people are not loved and accepted in spite of failures, they will soon learn to perform for men's praise rather than live to please God.

• Control your tongue and keep confidences. People who do not keep a confidence will not be confided in for long. Gossip kills trust, and without trust you have no basis for honest fellowship.

• Work toward a common goal. As ambassadors for Christ we want people to know us not only for our stand against worldliness, but also for our godly lifestyle.

## 3. Avoid the obvious obstacles that interfere with fellowship.

• Fellowship is based upon relationships which bloom into friendships. Relationships and friendships demand time commitments that are sometimes inconvenient sacrifices. Genuine fellowship is worth the cost; remember, people are more important than your schedule.

• Christian living is a family affair. As members of God's eternal family, we must work together and not compete against each other.

• Know-it-alls are hard to live with. God still desires men and women who are faithful, available, and teachable. Christians have been called to service, not stardom. One must encourage an atmosphere in which people are free to ask questions and receive answers that are not condescending.

• Refuse to show partiality. Partiality is not only selfishly motivated, it creates an unbiblical caste system which makes a small handful of friends winners and the rest of God's children losers. Christians have no right to treat a fellow believer as anything other than valuable.

## Conclusion

Our need for fellowship is great. The caring, sharing, giving, encouraging, exhorting, and self-sacrifice involved in biblical fellowship are necessary for our spiritual health. Our relationships within the body of Christ ought to be harbors of safety where a person can bare his soul and receive instruction, exhortation, care, prayer, and encouragement, not condemnation. The cost and effort required to overcome the obstacles to genuine fellowship are great, but the fruit that will be produced is well worth it. Are we willing to pay the price?

## CrossCheck

1. Why is fellowship an essential building block in the life of a Christian?

2. What does the author mean by creating a "safe harbor," and why is that important for experiencing fellowship?

3. "Most Christians are not experiencing Christian fellowship." Do you agree or disagree with this statement? If you agree, why do you think this is so?

4. Which of the components of fellowship are you experiencing in your church? Which are lacking? What can you do to promote the development of those that are lacking?

**Karl I. Payne** is minister of leadership development and responsible for discipleship and small groups at Antioch Bible Church in Kirkland, Washington. He is a graduate of Western Seminary in Portland, Oregon, and teaches at the seminary's extension school in Seattle. Karl is the author of *A Just Defense*.

CHAPTER 7

# Evangelism

*Joseph C. Aldrich*

**A** legend recounts the return of Jesus to glory after his time on earth. The angel Gabriel approached him and said, "Master, you must have suffered terribly for men down there." "I did," he said. "And," continued Gabriel, "do they know all about how you loved them and what you did for them?" "Oh, no," said Jesus, "not yet. Right now only a handful of people in Palestine know." Gabriel was perplexed. "Then what have you done to let everyone know about your love for them?"

Jesus said, "I've asked Peter, James, John, and a few more friends to tell other people about me. Those who are told will in turn tell still others, and my story will be spread to the farthest reaches of the globe. Ultimately, all of mankind will have heard about what I have done."

Gabriel looked rather skeptical. He knew well what poor stuff men were made of. "Yes," he said, "but what if Peter and the others grow weary? What if the people who come after them forget? Haven't you made any other plans?"

And Jesus answered, "I have no other plans. I'm counting on them." Twenty centuries later, he still has no other plan. He's counting on you and me. High on God's "To Do" list is the evangelization of the world. His early disciples adopted his priorities and devoted themselves to reaching their world. Christ counted on them, and they delivered. Have we done as well?

"But I'm not gifted for evangelism," you say. "I've tried

to use the popular methods. They don't work for me. If you're planning on telling me I can get to like them, don't bother. I've tried—honestly, I have—and I've fallen flat on my face. What can you say that will make a difference?"

You'll be delighted to know that we won't be talking about "the same song, second verse" approaches to evangelism. We'll be talking about touching people in ways appropriate to your own giftedness. I'm convinced that God is not so much asking you to tell others what a friend they have in Jesus as in showing them first what a friend they have in you.

Could a well-cooked meal sprinkled with lots of love start a people-flow toward the Cross? Can you bake a cherry pie? Part of preparing to become a redemptive person is growing in your understanding of how God draws people to himself. If you and I were neighbors committed to reaching our cul-de-sacs for Christ, what would we do? If we were committed to seeing our fellow employees come into God's family, where would we start? What plan would we follow, what tools would we use? Yes, the Bible is an essential tool, but I'm also talking about using your hammer and saw, your visegrips and your level. I'm talking about reaching folks through a well-cooked meal, a listening ear, a serving heart.

Luke tells us about a time when the Lord split up seventy-two of his disciples and sent them out. Spiritual training wheels in place, thirty-six rag-tag teams ventured out to extend the kingdom of light over the kingdom of darkness. How did they do? Luke 10:17 records that they proclaimed the gospel and "returned with joy."

It's a long, hard road from fear to joy. But be encouraged—we, too, can be used to bring people to Christ. Plugging in where God has gifted us to fit is what it's all about. Isn't it about time we got back to the Bible's way of moving people toward the Christ of the Cross?

### Cashing in on Your Networks

As I headed toward campus, I prayed, "Lord, send some searching nonbelievers my way." Being president of a Bible college has greatly limited my contact with the lost, and I guess my prayer came out of frustration. I long to share Christ with those who haven't discovered him. Little did I know that God would answer my prayer the very next day.

There was a knock on the door.

"Come on in," I said. The door opened, and there stood a giant of a man dressed in a wool shirt, faded work jeans, and heavy-duty suspenders. Well-worn logging boots completed his outfit. At first I didn't recognize this reincarnation of Paul Bunyan, but when I heard his voice, I knew. He was one of my old high school buddies from the 1950s. I hadn't seen him in almost thirty years.

"Bob, what in the world are you doing here?"

"Haven't the slightest idea, Joe. I was driving down Glisan Street, saw the 'Multnomah School of the Bible' sign, and the next thing I knew I had pulled my truck onto the campus. I walked into the closest building and asked the girl at the desk about Multnomah. She told me all about your college, and then mentioned that Joe Aldrich was president. I said, 'You mean Joe Aldrich from Vancouver, Washington?' She nodded, pointed down the hall, and said 'His office is right down there.'"

"So, what's going on in your life?" I asked with great anticipation. I remembered my prayer. Obviously Bob was the answer! The Lord had sent him my way, and it was my job to get him saved.

He explained how his marriage was falling apart and his world was caving in. He was in trouble. I had the answer. I backed up the evangelical dump truck and pulled the lever. I kept the heat on until he prayed the prayer. I gave him a new Bible, some quick words of assurance, and sent him on his way with the understanding he'd give me a call and we'd "get together sometime." I never heard from him again.

Bob wasn't ready, and I wasn't sensitive. I have no question that if I'd listened to him, entered into his pain and met with him as a friend and confidant, he'd have come to a genuine faith in Christ. But that's not what happened. I wanted immediate results; he wanted someone to listen and care.

I pray for Bob, that my stupidity will not hinder him from one day discovering the only answer to his pain and hurt. One thing's for sure: I made his pilgrimage to the Cross more difficult for the next person who attempts to point him in that direction.

Why do I tell that story? First, to remind you that no one bats a thousand when it comes to reaching souls. We all have our failures, even those who have reputations as "successful" soul winners. Second, through a negative example I want to highlight one of the Lord's primary strategies: Concentrate your evangelistic efforts on those who are ready.

## The Mission of the Seventy

Let's look a bit closer at the Lord's instructions to that band of disciples he sent out (Luke 10:1-24). The boys were sent out with three crucial instructions. They were to *search*, they were to *gain acceptance*, and they were to *stay where they found hospitality*. Their first goal was to discover open channels for the gospel.

In Matthew 10, Christ sent out the Twelve with the command to search for a "worthy" man and a "worthy" home. In Luke's account, the seventy were to look for a "man of peace." The twelve and the seventy were to look for worthy men and men of peace because the Lord knew these people would be most receptive to the gospel. The "man of peace" is likely to be more open than a "man of strife." It is probable that his family will also be inclined to respond.

The mission of the seventy encourages us to search for a point of receptivity. We don't confront the "impersonal community" with a frontal attack and hope someone, somewhere, weakens. While we want to work with people at all stages of readiness, it makes sense to focus on those we believe to be the most ready. Such people are "near." It makes sense to prequalify our audience.

Often our contribution is to discover the people responsive to us and our gifts, establish a redemptive relationship with them, and prepare them for the gifts of another believer who can lead them to Christ. Your contribution may be to find those who are open and then bring them under the ministry of those who are gifted in reaping.

"But," you ask, "what about those who are led to Christ by a stranger on an airplane? Or what about those who find Christ through a home visit by a stranger? They don't pre-qualify their audiences." That's true. I can't argue with that. We must be prepared to give the gospel to those we don't know. Some, however, are particularly gifted for those circumstances. Most are not.

### The *Oikos* Perspective

Although evangelism is personal in response, it is not individual in focus. Every individual must make a personal decision, but no individual should be viewed in isolation. In other words, I don't go out to "pick off" individuals. I claim entire networks.

Each of us has a circle of influence or a network made up of people related to one another through birth, career, or common interests, a social system made up of those who are in regular contact with each other through common ties and activities—neighbors, families, relatives, and coworkers.

I visualize the gospel flowing down these webs of relationships, reaching individual after individual who know and are somehow related to each other. This requires an *"oikos* perspective." *Oikos* is a Greek word for "household." An *oikos,* therefore, is a social system built around family and friends. Through these access doors you can build relationships with non-Christians.

### Implications of the *Oikos* Perspective

This biblical emphasis on the *oikos* as a center for evangelism implies several things. Let's look at some of them.

*1. For most of us, effective evangelism begins with networking.* Not all evangelism depends upon influencing social systems. A small percentage among us are especially gifted reapers.

But there is no reaping without cultivating and sowing. That's a reminder that we are laborers together with God. Soulcrafters don't solo. Sometimes a neighborhood network is a good place to start.

I was speaking in Colorado, and after the service, a young woman approached and asked, "Joe, do you remember me?" I didn't. I told the truth. "Well, I used to baby-sit your son." *Oh, that's right. But that was ten years ago!*

"I want you to know that two years ago someone shared Christ with me, and I became a believer. But the reason I trusted Christ was because of what I saw ten years ago. When I used to walk across the green strip of grass between your house and mine, it was like going from darkness to light. I couldn't figure out what made your home and family so different from mine. After I put your boy to bed, I used to go into the den and pull books off the shelf to try to find out what made you tick. When I'd leave your house to return home, it was like going from light back to darkness again."

Then she asked a very perceptive question. "Is that why you used to wax my dad's car?"

Her dad loved automobiles but couldn't do much to maintain them because of a heart condition. I'd learned that if you love what somebody else loves, you'll be loved. That's just what happened. I'd ask her father to give me his car keys, then I'd wash and wax his auto. He'd pull up a folding chair and we'd talk and talk. Not about spiritual things. He wasn't ready. His family was part of our neighborhood network, and we did lots of things together.

I'm delighted to report that the gospel has gone down through webs of relationships into that family unit. It started with a can of wax, a listening ear, and a curious baby-sitter. My prayer is that the entire *oikos* will be saved.

*2. A networking strategy will influence your approach to evangelism.* Reaching an *oikos* takes time. It takes preparation. It may take years of faithful prayer and service before a redemptive people-flow begins in your vocational network.

But it's unlikely to happen at all if you don't make it your goal.

Two of my pre-Christian friends are avid duck hunters. The Portland area's regional director for the Fellowship of Christian Athletes also hunts. My goal is to get them all together around something we share in common, and let God work through our association. It's a natural "hookup." The fact that my FCA friend was also an All-Pro football player adds another dimension.

3. *To influence networks, you must reach individuals.* My wife and I are praying that God will allow us to see six people from our networks trust Christ this year. Having identified those we believe to be the most responsive, we anticipate that the Lord, our colaborer, will work in and through us to bring insight, conviction, and new birth to our as-yet-unsaved friends.

## The Discovery Principle

You are the message. Those who respond to you socially will be open to you spiritually. Their reception of Christ often depends upon their reception of you. *No one will receive Christ through you who will not receive you first.*

Where do you go from here? First, identify your networks. To what groups, clubs, or associations do you belong? Who would be most receptive within these networks? Think of contacts within that *oikos* who would qualify as "worthy men and women." Jot them down. Second, begin to pray that God will use you in your present networks and that he will help you to build new ones.

"Charity begins at home," an old saying goes. I'm not sure I like the idea, but it might grow on me if we changed it to evangelism begins at home...especially in your "home neighborhood." Which *oikos* in yours looks ready?

### Knowing What to Say

Let's assume that you've discovered a worthy man or woman. He or she has welcomed you into their life. You have uncovered someone who will be spiritually responsive. What's next? Generally it is time to ask some key questions which test the water.

*The Pilgrimage Question.* There is no magic question, but I've found this one helpful: "Bill, we've never had a chance to talk about your religious background. At what point are you in your spiritual pilgrimage?"

The pilgrimage question is general enough to allow a response without embarrassment. No one likes to be put on the spot. This question allows your friend to choose a response appropriate to his comfort zone. His answer can be as simple or profound as he desires it to be.

The chief advantage of the pilgrimage question is that it gives you one final time for spiritual appraisal. As you listen carefully to the response, you make the final decision as to whether or not to share the gospel of saving grace at this time.

A related question is also helpful: "In your spiritual pilgrimage, have you come to the point of a personal commitment to Jesus Christ, or are you still on the way?" I've had many respond to this question by saying, "I'm still on the way." If that's their response, I'll usually say, "Well, Bill, maybe the next step God has for you is coming to understand how to establish a personal, saving relationship with him."

*Opportunity Statement.* Because the purpose of the pilgrimage question is to give nonbelievers the opportunity to pour out their religious beliefs, feelings, and concerns first, I usually find that little time is left for me to talk. Consequently, I plant seeds to prepare for a later discussion. I find it helpful to move from the pilgrimage question to this *opportunity statement*: "Sometime I'd like the opportunity to share four principles that will help you to understand what it means to have a personal relationship with Christ." A little later in the conversation I might reinforce this by saying, "Bill, I can understand your rejection of religion, with all its formality and hypocrisy. When I get an opportunity to share those principles with you, they should help answer your questions."

In some conversations I have dropped the idea of a further discussion five or six times. The response to this repeated suggestion must be observed and properly interpreted. It becomes your red or green light.

*Interest Question.* As the initial discussion time closes, it is often helpful to change the opportunity statement into a *question:* "Could I share those four principles with you?" This polite offer now allows your listener to talk. It is his turn to respond.

*Schedule Question.* If the response is positive to the interest question, schedule becomes the next focal point. Do you share the principles now or later? If later, some *scheduling questions* are important. "What's the best time for us to get together? Is morning okay for you?" Once a time is agreed upon...rejoice! Harvest is scheduled. A beginning as new as birth itself is about to take place.

*Gospel Explanation.* With a scheduled time and place, the next step is the *gospel explanation.* At this point the gospel itself (those four principles or whatever explanation of the gospel you prefer) is explained. The last section of this chapter describes how to summarize and present the gospel.

*Decision Questions.* Once the gospel has been clearly set forth, the *decision questions* are the next logical step. Here we are simply asking the individual to personalize the truth. I usually find the following three questions to be helpful:

1. Does this (the gospel) make sense to you?

2. On the basis of this (the gospel presentation) have you ever committed your life to Jesus Christ as your Savior?

3. Is there any reason why you wouldn't want to trust Christ right now?

Your friend is now at the point of decision. If he responds positively to the Spirit's wooing, he by faith will become a new creature in Christ.

The *pilgrimage question* is a spiritual litmus test. The *opportunity statement* is seed planting at its best (never underestimate the power of suggestion). It rouses curiosity and suggests a future course of action, a potential solution to some personal problems. The *interest question* is your way of determining whether your friend is open to and interested in pursuing conversation about the gospel. Assuming he is, the *schedule question* puts a definite time frame into the decision making process. "Sometime" becomes next Tuesday at 8:00 A.M. Then comes the *gospel explanation*, the *decision questions*, and the commitment to Christ!

Obviously, at any point in this communication sequence, the response could be negative. Your friend may express an interest in hearing those mysterious four principles, but be hesitant when you start talking schedule. Don't panic. Praise God he's expressed an interest in discussing spiritual things. Back off, continue to be his friend, and wait for another opportunity. I actually had a neighbor call me up and say, almost in desperation, "Joe, you've got to share those principles with me." I did. He's now a brother in Christ.

As a person approaches a decision for Christ, a major key is confidence. Believe, indeed expect, the individual will trust the Lord. You've seen him at work in your friend's life as you've spent time together. It's time to anticipate the rejoicing of angels in heaven! Fully expect God to bring the person to a point of salvation.

So what do you do before your scheduled appointment? Begin by praying a lot. Although God uses human agency, it is God who draws people to himself. But don't forget . . . you are important to the process. Then, if you haven't learned a good, logical gospel presentation, learn one. You may be saying, "I don't like methods. I prefer to just trust the Spirit of God." The fallacy of this reasoning is that "no method" is a method. It's the "no method" method. It's the "hamburger in the fan" approach to communication.

The Holy Spirit puts no premium on lack of preparation or shoddy thinking. Whatever else may be said, God is not the author of confusion. A carefully thought through presentation communicates to the listener that the message is important and worthy of his attention.

### Principles for a Personal Gospel Presentation

Before looking at the actual sharing process, let's consider a few foundational communication principles.

The effective evangelist *establishes a supportive, nourishing climate for communication.* A caring, sensitive manner is vital for sharing the good news. The unbeliever is not an enemy and you must not seek a decision in a battleground mindset. The goal is to win friends, not arguments. Sharing Christ is not something we do to an unbeliever as an object; it is something we do with an unbeliever as his friend and guide.

The effective evangelist *communicates empathy by asking questions and listening carefully.* The effective evangelist uses empathy to help discover the unbeliever's problems and devise gospel solutions. People are not afraid to believe, but they are afraid of being "sold." Our questions not only help us uncover their concerns, but they convey that we care.

*Effective communication is marked by humility and gentleness.* If you don't know the answer to a question, admit it. Don't assume an "I know everything" attitude. The goal is not to smother the unbeliever with facts. Often we try to communicate too much too fast.

Let's assume you are with your friend and are ready to move from the normal small talk to spiritual things. How do you do it? The following suggestions are just that—suggestions. You will have to develop a gospel presentation which is comfortable to you.

### Presenting the Gospel

*A transition.* The first challenge you face is to change the conversation to spiritual things. A good transition is the key. Campus Crusade for Christ has one I use often. "Just as there are physical laws which govern the universe, there are spiritual laws which govern our relationship with God. Bill, I'd like to share four of these principles with you." I often explain that whether or not I believe in the law of gravity, if I jump off a building, I'll become a believer. Whether I recognize it or not, our universe is controlled by physical and spiritual laws. My denial of these facts does not change the reality of them.

*Paper and pencil.* I prefer to actually write out the four laws (basics of the gospel) on a piece of paper. There are many advantages to this. It is more personal than reading from a booklet and it focuses attention on what you are doing. It also enables you to personalize your presentation. You can add diagrams or illustrations. Finally, you can give the sheet to them when you're finished. It becomes a "birth certificate" for many of them. I've had people open their Bibles and show me their certificate years after I shared Christ with them.

*Hold the questions.* You've allowed your friend to describe his pilgrimage. You've asked questions and listened carefully. If a question comes up now, don't let it interrupt your train of thought. Instead, compliment your friend and make a suggestion: "Bill, that's a very perceptive question. Would it be okay to hold that question until I've finished sharing the rest of these principles? I believe your question will be answered. If not, I'd be happy to respond to it." A deferred question seldom comes up again when the gospel has been clearly presented. Sometimes it is impossible (and unwise) to defer a question. If that is the case, answer it briefly and move on.

*Read or quote the pertinent Scripture verses.* The Word is quick and powerful. Use it. Let your friend look on with you as you read. It will be a great joy as you experience the Spirit of God using his holy Word to direct people to Jesus Christ. Guard against using too much Scripture, however. Once you have made your point, move on. Also, use a modern translation your friend can understand.

*Plant seeds again.* Several times during the gospel presentation I like to suggest the expected action to be taken. "Bill, *when* you make a commitment to Christ, you will discover what it means to have the peace of God." "*When* you receive Christ you will find that God will help you in your family relationships." This lets your friend know what the expected action is. It conveys confidence on your part that he both needs to make this decision and that he will.

It is reasonable to expect a favorable response. Having cultivated a friendship and bathed it in prayer, what else should we expect? When you're standing knee-deep in a field ready for harvest, why be hesitant? Suggesting the action step several times also prepares the person for the coming call to commitment.

Another advantage to this "when you..." seed planting is that it builds your own confidence. For most Christians the hardest part of sharing the gospel is calling for a commitment. Seed planting makes it easier and less threatening to transition to this vital part of the gospel.

*Share personal experiences.* Avoid the "before Christ I was a revolting rat and now I'm a super saint" mentality. At best, only half of the statement is true. Authenticity is important. Share progress that you have made, but don't leave the impression you have arrived. That you are progressing towards a destination is good news to many. If they're really friends, they've already seen you spill your milk.

Experiences they can identify with are especially valuable. If your friend is struggling with the issue of trusting Christ, describe the fears and apprehensions you had as you approached this decision point (assuming you had them).

*Be natural.* I can't stress this enough. Relax. God draws people to himself...through you. Guard against getting too animated. This doesn't mean you need to be impassive and play it cool. Be yourself and talk with (not preach at, manipulate, or coerce) your friend. I am in no way suggesting that you be solemn or sanctimonious. Humor can be very effective as a tension reliever. Use it wisely. Tears? Why not. This is a joyous occasion. I often find myself shedding tears of joy. A prodigal son is coming home. Glory!

*Use repetition and review for impact.* Regardless of the plan you use, when you have finished one point, review it and move on to the next. "Bill, we've seen that God really does love you. You are special to him." When you move on to a third major point, quickly review the other two. This reinforces the truth and increases understanding.

*Adapt your presentation to his needs.* If your friend needs reassurance of God's love, spend more time making this point. If he is already broken by sin, don't belabor the issue. The person who knows little about Christ may need you to spend most of your time talking about the uniqueness of the Lord's person and work. For others who understand Christ's uniqueness but have never responded to him, most of your focus should be on their need to receive him as Savior.

Quotations and comments from notable scholars and leaders can make a powerful contribution. Start collecting and memorizing them. They are especially effective for the individual struggling with the intellectual integrity of a commitment to Christ. Josh McDowell's book, *Evidence that Demands a Verdict*, is full of valuable quotes.

*Present the opportunity to trust Christ.* The time has come to seek a commitment. The *decision questions* described earlier provide a helpful way to make this an effective, productive experience.

1. Does this make sense to you?

2. On the basis of this, have you ever committed your life to Jesus Christ as your Savior?

3. Is there any reason why you would not want to trust Christ right now?

The first question helps you know whether or not your friend understands the gospel. The second question provides you with your friend's evaluation of his relationship to Jesus Christ. The third question is particularly important. It does not ask if the person wants to receive Christ, a question that anticipates a yes or no answer. Instead, it asks if there is a *reason* why the unbeliever would not want to trust Christ.

You anticipate his fear. As you mention praying to receive Christ, many non-Christians panic. They haven't done much praying and fear embarrassment. I've found this to be helpful: "Bill, I've shared Christ with many people, and I've found they sometimes feel awkward praying. I can appreciate that. The words are not important—God knows your heart—but if it makes sense to you, I will pray out loud, and if what I pray expresses how you feel, why don't you pray out loud after me? Would that be all right?" If so, I usually lead in prayer, one phrase at a time. Often the individual adds comments of his own. These are precious moments. What a joy to lead your friend to Christ!

*Provide assurance and follow-up.* Most gospel presentations have some simple thoughts to assure the individual of the reality of the new birth. I will not repeat them here. Follow-up is a delight because friends enjoy being together. Again, there are many helpful follow-up books available. Check with your pastor for a suitable one.

Where do you go from here? Out to love a friend to Christ, of course. You'll never have time if I keep writing. I'll quit writing about evangelism so you can start doing it. See you in glory. Introduce me to your neighbors when we get there. By God's grace you'll meet some of mine.

## CrossCheck

1. What does the author mean when he says we should use a hammer and saw or a well-prepared meal to win our neighbors to Christ? How does his perspective differ from those who advocate a "social gospel"?

2. What is the *oikos* perspective and what does it have to do with evangelism?

3. "No one will receive Christ through you who will not receive you first." Do you agree or disagree with that statement? Why?

4. Have you discovered a "worthy" man or woman among your friends, coworkers, or neighbors? What is your next step in pointing him or her to the Savior?

**Joseph C. Aldrich** is president of Multnomah Bible College in Portland, Oregon, and a graduate of Dallas Theological Seminary. He is the author of *Life-Style Evangelism*; *Gentle Persuasion: Creative Ways to Introduce Your Friends to Christ*; and *Prayer Summits*.

CHAPTER 8

# Discipleship
*Howard G. Hendricks*

I f you're serious about being a disciple of Jesus Christ, this book was designed for you. It has your name written all over it. It was also designed to help you disciple others. The order is significant: first you, then others. The focus of this concluding chapter is to encourage you to use what you've learned in the previous chapters to begin discipling others.

I'm convinced that the greatest need of the contemporary church is an understanding of and involvement in the disciplemaking process. The greatest threat to Christianity is Christians, trying to sneak into heaven incognito, without ever sharing their faith, without ever becoming involved in the most significant work on earth. I want to try and make sure that never happens to you.

## What Is a Disciple?

By the time you get through this chapter, I hope you wonder if you are a disciple. That will be a healthy response. But what a disciple *is* will determine what a disciple *does*. Let's look at some yardsticks by which to measure not only whether you are a discipler, but also whether you are a disciple.

## A Disciple Is a Learner

Jesus said, "Take my yoke upon you and learn from me" (Matt. 11:29). The meaning of the Greek word for "disciple" is *learner*. That means the disciple is teachable. Are you? I would rather disciple a person who did not know *schmatz* who has all the answers but is not learning. If you stop studying and learning today, you stop discipling tomorrow.

The church biblically conceived is a school. It's a place where Christians are equipped, trained. It is not a place to come and be entertained. It is not a place to come and watch a pro do his thing and give him a hand.

Jesus was never hung up over the fact that his disciples didn't know everything. "I have a lot of things to share with you, but you're not able to bear it now. But that's no problem because when the Spirit of truth comes, he'll guide you into all truth." Friend, you don't have to tell your disciples everything you know, now. Save a little for the next session.

A disciple, first of all, is a learner. Are you?

## A Disciple Is a Follower

A disciple is one who follows or imitates the life and teaching of another. The apostle Paul made a statement I will never forget. He said, "Follow me, as I follow Christ." Do you recoil from that? The first time I heard that verse I said, "You've got to be kidding! I'd never say that." It makes little difference whether you say it or not; that's exactly what's happening. *People are following you.* The question is, "Are you following Christ?"

The greatest means of communication is through modeling—not what you say but what you are. You can be a model even if you're very young. Paul knew young, timid Timothy was overwhelmed with his assignment to lead the church at Ephesus, so Paul galvanized him with this: "Don't let anyone look down on you because you are young, but set an example for the believers in speech, in life, in love, in faith and in purity" (1 Tim. 4:12). Then note verse 15, "Be diligent in these matters; give yourself wholly to them, so that everyone may see your *progress.*" That's the key. Paul's not talking about a perfect person, he's talking about a progressing person. He's not talking about a person who's arrived, he's talking about a person who's en route.

A man in Indianapolis taught me an important lesson a number of years ago. He was extremely effective not only in leading people to Christ but in building them up in the faith. One of the first things he does after he leads a person to Christ is suggest they have lunch together. So they get together for lunch and he asks, "How's it going?" "Great! It's wonderful to know Jesus and have my sins forgiven." "Having any problems?" "No, everything's just great!" "Would you mind if I shared one of my problems with you?" "You have a problem? But you led me to Christ!"

Right from the start, he communicates that a Christian is not a person without problems. He is a person with the problem-solver living within him.

## A Disciple Is a Reproducer

Discipleship is never an end in itself, it is always a means to an end. God is not building into your life to end the process there; he's building into your life in order to multiply through your life. That again is the problem in our churches. We're leading people to Christ but they're not reproducing. In the average evangelical church you cannot find 10 percent who are consistently leading people to Jesus Christ, much less building them up in the faith. A lot of Christians are scared to death at the thought of sharing their faith.

Those involved in discipleship ministries often talk about "training" individuals. But what does it mean to train someone? When have you trained a person? *You have not trained someone until you have equipped him to do for others what you have done for him.* Did you teach him how to lead somebody to Christ? That's not training. He is trained when he can teach someone else how to lead someone to Christ.

I've had six courses in personal evangelism in my education, and not one of them has done a blessed thing for me. In one course we had a list of verses and a list of excuses to memorize. Then we went into Chicago to Union Station to do personal work, and the first person I sat next to brought up an excuse that wasn't on my list. I was hung! Memorizing those lists had not trained me to do evangelism.

There are some basic phases to training reproducers. First is the *telling* phase, which involves ideally both written and spoken communication. But let's face it, if telling were training, most of our disciples would be brilliant. Telling is basic, but it doesn't end there. The next phase is *showing*. I not only need to read it and hear it, I need to see it being done. The final phase is *doing*, and ideally, it needs to be broken down into two parts. First, you need to do it *under a controlled situation*—that is, where you can fall flat on your face without losing face. And second, you need to do it *in a real life situation*. Only then can you say this person is trained, he is capable of reproducing.

How do you learn to preach? By preaching. How do you learn to do personal evangelism? By doing personal evangelism. How do you learn to study the Bible? Not by listening to pros teach it but by getting your nose in it, by hitting your head against an interpretive problem, by coming up with all kinds of questions.

I've never yet heard of a correspondence course in swimming. You don't learn to swim by reading books about swimming or even by watching the pros going up and down in the pool. You learn to swim by diving in, splashing away like crazy until you finally begin to get some coordination into the strokes. That's what discipleship is all about.

A disciple, then, is a *learner*; therefore, perpetuate the learning process in your life and in the life of your disciple. A disciple is a *follower*; therefore, make sure you provide adequate models. They are going to follow you. Are you following Christ? A disciple is a *reproducer*; therefore, be careful how you build because you are going to have to live with your product.

### The Biblical Model for Discipleship

Making disciples is not an option. It is an essential, a biblical mandate. Jesus makes that unmistakably clear in the passage often referred to as the Great Commission:

Then Jesus came to them and said, "All authority in heaven and on earth has been given to me. Therefore go and make disciples of all nations, baptizing them in the name of the Father and of the Son and of the Holy Spirit, and teaching them to obey everything I have commanded you. And surely I am with you always, to the very end of the age" (Matt. 28:18-20).

The apostle Paul caught the vision for disciplemaking and sums it up in these instructions to his disciple Timothy:

And the things you have heard me say in the presence of many witnesses entrust to reliable men who will also be qualified to teach others (2 Tim. 2:2).

So the Scriptures leave no doubt that we are to be about this business of making disciples. Furthermore, the Bible provides us with a model for disciplemaking. Before Jesus Christ ever commanded his followers to make disciples, he had built into the lives of those men through a distinctive discipling process. He gave them a model before he gave the mandate. The same is true of the apostle Paul—before he *told* Timothy, he *trained* Timothy.

Your disciples, like my students, will not necessarily do what you say. They will tend to do what you do. Some years ago, I became interested in small group involvement and wanted to communicate this to my students. But instead of instructing them in small group techniques, I would say at the beginning of a class, "All right, gentlemen, the first thing we are going to do today is to divide up into groups. I want you five guys to move over here, you five back there," and so on. Later I went out to the churches where these students were ministering, and lo and behold, they'd get up and say, "Now, ladies and gentlemen, the first thing we're going to do tonight is divide up into groups. I want you five people to go over here..." I never told them to do that. They were doing what I was doing, not what I was telling them to do.

As I wander all over the landscape, I am constantly taking students with me. I teach a student more between Dallas and Oklahoma City and between Oklahoma City and Dallas than I sometimes do in four years in the classroom. And long after that student has graduated, he'll say to me, "Prof, do you remember the trip to Oklahoma City? Boy, that's where God broke through to me." You know why? Because more is caught than taught. But if a person never gets close enough to feel your heartbeat, to find out your value system, to discover what you are committed to, then it's a little hard for this to rub off. About all they pick up are your words, and most of us are weary of words.

You know what most of us are doing? We are overtraining our disciples. Too often we give the impression that unless you know everything perfectly, you are not prepared to do anything for Jesus Christ. Nothing could be further from the truth. Paul trained Aquila and Priscilla for eighteen months, and he determined they were ready to carry on a significant ministry of their own.

A student came up after class one day and said, "Prof, can you give me something that's a little more challenging?" I said, "Yeah, I think I've got something for you." I sent him out to this fraternity house to do a little evangelism, and they plastered the walls with the guy. The student who picked him up said, "I couldn't believe it; he was white as a sheet."

He came to me later and said, "Prof, I want you to pray for me." "Great, what do you want me to pray for?" "Pray they won't go for my throat." "You know I won't pray for that. That's exactly what I *will* pray for." The next morning I met him on campus, and said, "How did it go?" He said, "The Lord answered your prayers." Greatest thing that ever happened to him.

Now let me nail something in your thinking. The early days in a person's life are determinative physically and emotionally. Those early hours, early days, early years are strategic in marking a child for life. That's no less true in the spiritual realm, and it's why discipleship is so critical. What you expose a new disciple to early in his Christian life will mark him. Paul had a tremendous burden to tell Timothy to pass on to others what he had been taught because that's exactly what happened to him when he came to faith. That's why it's so critical in the early stages of a new believer's Christian life to get him into memorizing the Word, studying the Scriptures, sharing his faith, and teaching him some basic principles of Christian experience.

## Selecting Disciples

But how did Jesus choose his disciples? For years I have been intrigued by his choice of material. It's such a stark contrast to the way I choose mine. I choose men because I like them; they're my kind. I love to hand-pick a winner; I don't want to associate with a loser. Second, I choose a man because he likes me, he appreciates me, he thinks my ministry is very effective (you know, a perceptive man with a great deal of discernment). Third, I choose someone because he is like me. I'm an extrovert, and if you're a horseradish man, then you choose that kind of individual.

That's how I naturally tend to select disciples. But are there any clues in the Gospels that provide a better pattern? I think there are, and I want to focus our attention on a passage in the Gospel by Luke—Luke 6:12-19.

### Basic Principles for Selecting Disciples

The first principle is the obvious but neglected principle of *prayer*. Only after an entire night in prayer did Jesus choose his disciples. At every crucial point in his life, Jesus spent a considerable time in prayer. Saturate your choices with prayer. And bear in mind that you must make choices; you cannot disciple everyone. Jesus didn't.

Jesus did not begin his disciplemaking by saying, "Now, the first thing you need to know is to pray. It's important to pray—it's your spiritual lifeline." He never said that. He just prayed. And every time they sent out a search party, they found him on his knees. Finally they got the message: "Prayer is important," and they asked the Lord to teach them to pray.

There's another reason to pray about whom you should

select as a disciple. The fact is, you may have some failures. Jesus had one. He prayed all night and chose Judas. There are going to be some people into whose life you make the greatest investment who are going to disappoint. Prepare yourself for it. Unless you have saturated those choices in prayer, when they bomb out, you're going to be devastated.

Sometimes we have not come to grips with the realities of life. That's why I've discovered I have to spend more time in prayer, not only to help me make better decisions, but also if I make a decision that doesn't work out, I have some spiritual perspective. This really isn't my business, it's God's.

The second principle is *exposure*. Too often people have the impression that Jesus was walking down the road one day and said, "Follow me," and these men took off and followed him. Hardly. They had been exposed to Jesus, to his teachings and miraculous healings, long before he called them to be his disciples. They had a lot of time to observe him; he had a lot of time to observe them.

The third principle from this passage is *variety.* I believe this passage is teaching us to opt for diversity, not uniformity, in choosing disciples. You have never seen a wider collection of individuals than the twelve men Jesus chose. He chose a radical and he chose a redneck. He chose extroverts and he chose introverts. Some of them never peeped—you'll search all over the place trying to find two statements they made. And then there's Peter... Jesus chose leaders and he chose followers. He chose some gifted men, he chose some limited men; he chose some bright men, he chose some with average intelligence.

Variety is the genius of the body of Christ. I used to try to get a group of men around me who were just like me. It didn't work. I once had a student in a discipleship group, and I thank God upon every remembrance of him. I don't think he made ten statements during the semester with the exception of the day he led the group and the times he prayed. I took an evaluation at the end of the semester and asked the group which member had made the greatest impact on them. You know who it was? That student with his ten statements. You have one on your church board, the person who sits there and never says anything; he just listens to everything that's going on. All of a sudden he opens his mouth, and when he does, you'd better listen. He's not going to say a whole lot, but when he does, it's going to be significant. Not like those of us who having nothing to say, and say it.

The last principle is *potential*. How you see your disciples will largely determine what they become. You see them as a problem? You may develop them into one. Some of us have grown in the faith because somebody saw beyond the superficial and anticipated what the grace of God could accomplish in us.

We had a student at the seminary a few years back whom I love like crazy. I told him one day I'd pay *him* tuition to come to class for what he did for me. I was out ministering somewhere and had used his testimony, and this couple came up afterwards and said, "You're sure you've got the right guy? He went to such and such a college?" "Right." "Ah, no way!" You see, he was the hell raiser at that school. A group of Christians on that campus got together one day and asked, "Who's the least likely to come into the kingdom of God?" They universally voted on the same man—this student.

One day I asked him, "How in the world did you ever make it?" He said, "Prof, you wouldn't believe a couple I met. They invited me over to their beautiful home, and I was so stupid, I came in cutoffs and bare feet. I was so filthy I even smelled to myself, but they just loved me for Jesus' sake. I used to ply them with all of my crazy philosophical questions. They just listened and heard me out and loved me. One day they said, 'You know, we've been praying for you, and we're convinced God has a great future for you.' I didn't sleep for sixteen nights in a row until I came kicking and screaming into the kingdom of God."

Now let's be honest. Suppose you were interested in launching a worldwide enterprise. Would you have picked the twelve disciples? I think most of us would have passed them by. You go down the list and you say, "Good night! Why did Jesus choose *them?*" For the same reasons you ought to be choosing people. You don't choose people on the basis of what they *are,* but on the basis of what they are *to become* by the grace of God working in you, working in them.

## Developing Disciples

After we've made that critical decision about whom we are going to disciple comes the equally critical question, "How do I develop these disciples? How do I build into their lives?"

There are two basic steps in making disciples. Your first task is to *determine what you want to develop.* It's important to have clearly in mind where you are going right at the outset of any undertaking. The reason we often feel we are doing so well is that we really don't know what we're doing. Once you have determined what it is you want to develop, then your second task is to *develop what you have determined.*

### Determine What You Want to Develop

So what is it we ought to be developing in the making of disciples? What ought we to be looking for in a disciple? I'm looking for three things. First, I am looking to develop a *committed individual,* a person who has made certain basic spiritual decisions. He has unreserved commitment to Jesus Christ and to the body of Christ. It's not sufficient to commit yourself to the Savior without committing yourself to the saints. There's no such thing as an independent Christian. I need you, you need me, we need each other.

We also need unreserved commitment to the ministry of God in the world. God didn't redeem you simply to provide an insurance policy to keep you out of hell. He saved you in order to make you like his Son, who so loved the world that he gave himself for it. Your primary purpose as a believer is to make an impact with that redeemed life upon this world.

The second thing I want to help develop is a *competent individual.* I'm looking for someone who *knows* something.

I also want that person to *feel* something. He is not merely passive about the truths he has learned. He's excited about them. Third, a competent person *does* something. A competent individual is a person who knows something fully, who feels something deeply, and who behaves something consistently. It's out of the overflow of that full life that he has something to minister to others.

The third thing I am looking for is a *creative individual.* I'm looking for someone who's able to think, not simply rearrange his prejudices. I'm looking for someone who can dream, who's convinced it hasn't all happened. I'm looking for someone who can believe God for his specialty—the impossible.

I'm looking for people who are committed, competent, and creative. Unfortunately, such people are hard to find—impossible, in fact. That's why you must develop them. But you can never develop committed, competent, creative disciples unless these are your goals. You achieve what you aim for.

### Develop What You Have Determined

After you have determined what you want to develop, then develop what you have determined. How did Jesus go about developing his disciples? A study of the Gospels suggests four ways that are open to you as you build into the life of another.

First, *Jesus developed his disciples by example.* They observed him up close for three and a half years in every conceivable situation. There has to be some congruence between what a person learns from you and what he sees in your life. If what he sees is incompatible with what you tell him, then no matter how accurate, how biblical, how necessary the things you tell him, you do not communicate.

What Christ was to his disciples was far more important than what he said. As you trace through the Gospels, you discover half the time they forgot what he said—even the most elementary things. He had to repeat himself over and over again, and they still had a hard time getting the picture. But they never forgot what he was. His words were validated by his life. He was for real.

In Luke 6:40 Jesus makes a remarkable statement: "Everyone who is fully trained will be like his teacher." You are going to reproduce like kind. Do you like what you are? That's what you are going to reproduce.

But please note, there is one significant difference between you and your disciples and Jesus and his. Make sure you share your failures with your disciples. Jesus never did because he never failed, but that's not true of you or me.

A year ago I handed out some evaluation sheets to students and said, "Give me some constructive suggestions for this course. What is it that made it worthwhile taking this course?" Two-thirds of the students concurred, "One of the greatest contributions of this course was that you shared your failures." Your disciples will forgive you for your failures—they will probably respect you all the more for being real—but they will not forgive you for your dishonesty.

Second, *Jesus developed his disciples by problems.* We run from problems, but Jesus involved his disciples in the realities of life. Christian education is entirely too passive. We have too many spectators. Jesus trained his disciples on the battlefield, not by removing them from the battle.

In Mark 4 we find a series of lectures on faith by the world's greatest teacher. But Jesus knew you cannot communicate faith by a series of lectures, so he puts the disciples into a laboratory and begins by giving them a hearing test. He says, "Gentlemen, let's go over to the other side of the lake." "Roger!" So off they go.

Soon after the boat is in the water, water is in the boat, and this group of professional fishermen begins to panic. They'd never seen a storm like this one, and they come to Jesus and say, "Teacher, don't you care if we drown?" The implication is, "At least you could help us bail!"

So the Lord gets up and rebukes the wind and waves, no problem there. Then he turns to the disciples and asks, "How is it that you of all people have no faith?" The men who had just heard the lectures on faith got a big fat "F" on this test, and it didn't stand for Faith. Jesus had said, "Let us go over to the other side," not "Let us go to the middle of the lake and drown." They flunked the hearing test. If Jesus says, "We're going to the other side," *we're going to the other side.*

What are you doing to develop the faith of your disciples? They won't develop it by having you lecture them from your set of notes from Faith 101. That s not how they learn.

Third, *Jesus developed his disciples by love.* Have you ever asked why men followed Jesus, what was the magnetism of his life? Jesus loved his disciples, and a lover is a leader. The early church developed a reputation, even among the pagans, for how they loved one another. Jesus Christ conveyed that love to his disciples just as you and I have to convey it to our disciples in ways they can understand.

Fourth, *Jesus also developed his disciples by trusting.* The secret of making disciples is developing confidence in the Spirit's ability to change a person. If you're going to minister and develop faith, you're going to have to communicate your confidence in the Lord working in the disciple's life. When you begin to see what God is able to do in your disciples' lives, your ministry will be transformed.

Too often we look at our disciples and say, "I don't know what God could do with him; he's not much of a public speaker. And this one, he has a hard time even relating to people. And this one over here has such a short fuse, and this one has a trashed-up marriage. We're never going to make it!" You're displaying your unbelief. God wants to move into the life of each individual with whatever limitations, whatever problems, whatever gifts, whatever assets he has, and use him as a sharp instrument in his hands.

You want to pray for something rare, something you won't see much of? Ask God to give you spiritual discernment—to see beyond where the person is right now, to what he may become by the grace of God.

I had a student a few years ago, and I used to wonder

what in the world was going to become of him. He slept through most classes; he might as well have slept through all of them. He finally graduated—how, I'll never know—and took a church in Canada that seventeen men in a row had walked away from. When I heard what he'd done I thought, *That's par for the course. He doesn't know enough not to take it.*

He took the church, and it wasn't long before a crisis came. A dear man in the church lost his wife and four children in an automobile accident. This man called and said, "Pastor, the Lord's taken my entire family to be with himself." My former student hung up the phone and thought, *I've got to go over there. But what in the world am I going to say?* He stayed away as long as he could and finally went over, only to find this layman ministered to him. The young man had nothing to say.

That's when God broke through in his life. He began to preach the Word. He began to go out with laymen, training them, sharing Christ. He didn't know how to do it himself, so he was learning en route. And that church began to see people respond to the Savior. Wherever I went across the country, I kept hearing about him. I'd ask, "Are you sure you have the right name? Spell it!"

One day he wrote me, "I understand you're coming to our area. Would you come and preach for my people? I'd love for them to hear you." I wrote back and said, "I'd love to preach for you and see the work you're involved in." When I walked into this church, the place was jammed to the doors. It was so crowded the people were standing around the back, and when I got up to preach, I gave someone my seat. After I finished preaching, a deacon came up and said, "That's pretty good preaching, son, but have you ever heard our preacher preach?" I came back to seminary with a new lease on life.

My seminary colleagues and I have set no track record for determining who will be successful. We can't make those determinations. Neither can you. Unless God is working through you, and particularly in the life of your disciples, you are laboring in vain, and God is not about to share his glory with you or anyone else.

It's a miracle God wants to use you and me, and it's a miracle he wants to use any of our disciples. But it's exactly what he wants to do. Stop feeling sorry for yourself that you're a carpenter or an engineer or a housewife. Your ministry is to reach carpenters, engineers, or housewives. Some of the best people to win lawyers are lawyers. Some of the best people to reach housewives are housewives. Did it ever occur to you why God placed you in the community in which you live? That wasn't by accident either. "I'm the only person on this block who knows Jesus." Fantastic! Just think of it. God entrusted the whole block to you! *God hand-picked you to be his representative to this generation.*

I hope you never recover from that. Friends, may all of us never recover together.

### CrossCheck

1. The author says the greatest need of the church is an understanding of and involvement in the disciplemaking process. Why do you think he says that is the greatest need? Do you agree with his assessment?

2. What are the marks or measuring sticks of a disciple? Which of those measuring sticks best characterizes your own discipleship? Which one is least characteristic of you?

3. One of Paul's more successful discipling ministries was with Aquila and Priscilla. What advantages are there in discipling couples? What might be some disadvantages?

4. Are you currently involved in a discipleship ministry with a couple or an individual? If so, what two or three principles from this chapter can you begin using to make that relationship more effective? If you are not presently discipling someone, what are two or three reasons you've found in this chapter for beginning such a ministry?

**Howard G. Hendricks** is distinguished professor and chairman of the Center for Christian Leadership at Dallas Theological Seminary. He is the author of several books, including *Teaching to Change Lives* and *Heaven Help the Home.*